Forty Years
OF PMS

and Other Musings of an Aging Hippie

LINDA GOOR NANOS

Permission granted
Gifts From Eykis, Wayne W. Dyer, Copyright 1983, HarperCollins Publishers

Photo Editing by Laura Akscin Foord

FOREWARD

But for a chance tarot card reading, this book would not have been completed. I have had self-doubts and wondered why anyone would want to read this ordinary woman's story but I realized that my story is just a vehicle to talk about love, relationships, marriage, and facing and overcoming hardships. I may not be Every Woman, but there are parts of me in every woman.

This book is dedicated to my family, always at its center.

FORTY YEARS OF PMS
And Other Musings of an Aging Hippie

The Invitation

I sat on the edge of the examination table in my disposable medical gown, otherwise naked, with the opening to the front. It was my first appointment in a new gynecologist's office and an unsmiling nurse was writing down my medical history. She looked at me from behind her clipboard and tapped her pen on its hard surface.

"So you don't remember at what point your water broke with your first delivery?" she asked.

I modestly adjusted my paper garb to cut down on the icy draft as well as to avoid embarrassing exposure. The information she asked was most likely only retrievable by hypnosis; I couldn't recall facts about when, where, and how my water broke twenty-one years prior to that exam. I generally function on a need-to-remember basis, and this was not a fact I was likely to require in my day-to-day life and so it had been relegated to the most inaccessible archives of my mind.

"No, I'm sorry, I really can't recall," I eventually admitted. "It seems unimportant now, so many years later."

"Unimportant? I remember every detail of giving birth, to *all four* of my children."

Ugh. This was a close encounter with someone whom the author and humorist Erma Bombeck would refer to as a prime time mother who was easily identified by her maddening perfection. That would make me a not-ready-for-prime-time-mother, my worst fear.

I can't say I don't have any memories of the momentous event of my first child's birth because I do remember my husband having the idea that blackberry brandy would ease the pain of labor. The result of this home remedy was a purple projectile vomit that shot across the bed and landed on him. It was my own special way of thanking him for his contribution towards my condition, as well as for the home remedy. I also recall that we almost didn't make it to the hospital with my second child. Since my first labor of giving birth to my son lasted for eighteen hours that were agonizing for all concerned, we stalled the trip to the hospital with baby number two as long as possible. No blackberry brandy was offered that time. We waited so long to leave the house that I went into transition in the car and began to rant that he should pull over so that I could give birth on the side of the road. We made it to the hospital with barely enough time. Three pushes and my daughter was born.

After being criticized by this Nurse Ratched Wannabe for not recalling the particulars of childbirth two decades before, I punted her next question, "How old were you when you began to menstruate?" Surely, there could be no excuse for not knowing when I started menstruating.

"Twelve years old," I answered, thinking that was a fairly normal age for the onset of puberty. While I may not have remembered the exact age, it was circa 1964, and I could vividly picture being doubled over with cramps and having the following conversation with my older brother, Mark:

"I don't know why you are in so much pain. I read that a girl can swim and play tennis when she has her period."

"Oh, yeah, like you're now an authority on girls' periods! I saw you reading that on the back of a tampon box. Believe me, I'm not in any shape for diving into our pool!" I wished 40 years of periods on him at that very moment.

Mark shrugged his shoulders and walked away, probably to put some Clearasil on his pimples or Brylcreem on his hair. He was grappling with his own puberty issues: acne and a cow-licked crew cut.

When the nurse exited the room, I felt angry that I had allowed myself to be so intimidated by her. In my medical gown with bare feet dangling, my professional credentials as an attorney were inconsequential. It's not that I expected her to even the playing field by walking around in a paper gown with vital areas exposed, but she could have been more warm and fuzzy to a new patient.

I could hear the doctor's voice as he greeted the patient in the next room and then closed the door behind him. We were stacked up like flights waiting for departure on the tarmac. I passed the time waiting for him to arrive by reading an article on the wall: "Doctor by Day, Actor by Night." There were pictures of my new gynecologist playing Sky Masterson, the errant gambler in "Guys and Dolls." Who wouldn't want a doctor with great insights into his patients' motivations and the meaning of life? Was it all just a crap shoot or would we be saved and find higher callings? On the other hand, I was troubled by whether or not he would be thinking about casting calls while taking a Pap smear or rehearsing his current script while examining my breasts.

The doctor entered stage right and reported that the blood test that I had taken showed my hormone levels were "fully menopausal." I felt as if I had made it to the hormone finish line, except that instead of a medal around my neck or a trophy, my reward was night sweats and hot flashes. It was a pivotal point in my life. After forty years of menstruating, give or take a few estimated years, it was over. No more pads, tampons, or Midol; the feminine hygiene aisle in the pharmacy was now rendered irrelevant. But the pharmaceutical industry won't mourn the loss of this customer because the "cycle" will continue with some young pre-teen buying her first maxi pad. This young girl will not appreciate the advances that have been made in feminine hygiene.

When I was a teen, we anchored pads the size of blackboard erasers to ridiculous looking sanitary napkin belts with treacherous metal fasteners. As a little girl, prior to knowledge of menstruation, I saw Kotex boxes in the store with women in gowns on the front. Whatever was in those boxes I wanted, but my mother told me I couldn't buy one and the only explanation I was given was, "You are too young to understand." Once I needed to buy sanitary pads, I wanted nothing to do with them. I didn't appreciate the fact that the pads were actually an improvement over the personal hygiene of my grandmother's generation. They used old cloth cut into rags as pads; the expression "on the rag" lived on in the vernacular long after the mode of hygiene disappeared.

The sanitary pad was augmented by tampons, but you had to have a modern mom to be able to use them. Although, anyone who has inserted a tampon knows that there is nothing remotely sexual about the process of inserting one; some mothers told their daughters that tampons were for "fast girls," not wanting their daughters to corrupt their virginal state with intrusive absorbent cotton. Today, not only can you buy thin, self-adhesive pads, if you need there are pads designed to be worn with thong underwear or underwear that is itself moisture absorbent. Women have never had it so good! I regret that I will never experience a thong pad or space age technology underwear, but this deprivation is more than outweighed by not needing any pad at all.

I asked "Dr. Sky Masteron By Night" if this meant I could stop with my semi-annual pap smears or dispense with pelvic sonograms.

"Unfortunately, no. Please lay down with your feet in the stirrups and scoot down." I knew the drill all too well and it wasn't made any better by having a leading man poking and prodding my private parts. "Okay," he said, "everything feels normal. I'll see you back here in six months." As he exited stage left, I thought about my new stage of womanhood. The absence of a period is disconcerting at first; menstruation is something predictable in a world that is otherwise precarious and tenuous. Its presence was a constant reminder of the feminine identity that provided impetus throughout puberty, courtship, marriage, raising a family, and career. With menstruation behind me, it seems like an appropriate time to reflect on my journey of womanhood. There have been issues thrown at me like ground balls and pop flies that I was forced to field along the way.

I have found that the issues facing the female listeners who call into the radio program I tune into on the way to work are the same issues that I have confronted in my life. Each phase brought fresh challenges as a single woman, a new wife, an unskilled mother, a career woman juggling marriage and family, and an empty-nester wondering what the next forty years have in store for me. It is up to us well-cured women to provide the uninitiated the benefit of our experience and the perspective that comes with maturity.

We all marvel at how the beautiful and talented Meryl Streep ages so gracefully. Over time, she has been cast in more mature roles and always masters them. We all want to know how she manages to be so perfect. I have noticed there is a vigorous movement, perhaps an AARP conspiracy, to convince mature Americans that life, like Scotch in an oak cask, gets better with age. Some women may welcome a little mutual support. If you are among those of us who find the aging process and life's passages to be challenging, this book is for you.

How we view age, like Einstein's theory, is a matter of relativity. I realized I was getting old when I was looking at a ten-dollar bill and was struck by the exceptional good looks of one of our country's founding fathers, Alexander Hamilton. If I had been around in 1787, I would have checked out his constitution. It is true that age is all a point of perspective, but to those who say, "Fifty is just a number," I remind you it's also the age when many doctors recommend regular colonoscopies.

Life is not always glamorous and sometimes we face affronts by forces of fate and failures of free will. There are moments when I have felt isolated, or as Tennessee Williams described it, sentenced to solitary confinement within my own skin. While it may be true that nobody can experience life in exactly the same way, sharing does lighten the load. Though we may come from different walks of life and think that nobody understands our unique journey, Maya Angelou reminds us in her poem "Human Family," that people are more alike than unalike. Never was this truer than when we compare the challenges women face.

If I am guilty of seeking comradery out of my own needs, then let me make up for it by being a good hostess. Writing a book about my journey of womanhood is like that paper medical gown, a lot of exposure. I will think of it as a slumber party filled with laughter and solidarity. Bring your blanket, pillow, and favorite munchies because we may be up until the wee hours. There is so much to talk about! It's about the sharing. I'll go first, but remember, what happens in 40yrspms group, stays in 40yrspms group!

PART ONE

ONE

Warning: Adult Content

(SEXUAL SITUATIONS, DRUG USE, AND SOME NUDITY)

My image as a woman has been largely shaped and defined by marriage and family, albeit replete with role reversals, but the stages of my life before I set down the roots of monogamy and children were formative in terms of my identity as a sexual being. My pre-teen and teen years were not particularly promiscuous or experimental, though some overly imaginative twelve year old wrote, "Linda Gore is a Hore" on the back of a school bus seat in Magic Marker. My maiden name lent itself to that clever rhyme. He was neither a gentleman nor a scholar. Even my name was misspelled. For the record, it was all about the rhyme and I was very chaste.

As a pre-pubescent, I played spin the bottle and cringed with the rest of my friends when the bottle pointed to a guy whom we called "Soggy Lips." I found an old diary that I kept when I was twelve years old. One entry reads, "I went to a dance. We were dancing with the boys, talking with them and they were even buying us refreshments." Life doesn't get much better than that! There were many hearts drawn with a litany of names, all followed by the inscription "4 Ever." I was fortunate that I was not of age to get tattoos because all of those hearts could have amounted to a terrible amount of tattoo regret. While I may have been boy crazy, all things considered, I was not on the fast track.

I remember one poor gal in junior high who had the unfortunate last name "Moore" and was referred to as "Gives More." Since her name stuck, while the rhyme about my name didn't, I can assume there was some truth in it. "Which gal had been felt up" was always a headline with "who went all the way" being the feature story. The fact that I made it through high school a virgin I attribute to my being clueless.

One heartthrob broke up with me every Friday so he wouldn't have to date me on the weekends when he played with his band and had groupies following him. I didn't complain because I was dating the lead singer of the band Monday through Friday. The other high school boyfriend made some attempts at seduction, but I didn't know what he was trying to accomplish. He must have felt that taking me to the prom was a total waste of a tuxedo when it didn't get him to home plate.

Everything went haywire when I attended the State University of New York at Albany during the early seventies. It was the height of sex, drugs, and rock 'n roll. Let me hit "Pause" for a moment to remind relatives, friends, and co-workers that this Chapter, covering the hippie years, is rated "Adult Content." You may wish to "Fast Forward" to Chapter Two, which is rated PG-13.

In college, casual sex became the mode; AIDS and safe sex were not yet a part of our societal consciousness. One evening at the campus Rathskeller, a male friend began to flirt with me. The floors were already sticky with spilled beer by the time he made it around to me. He was wearing the uniform: denim jeans, a flannel shirt, and hiking boots that most likely had never touched a trail. His curly locks brushed his skinny shoulders.

"I haven't seen you lately. You're looking *really* good," he said.

"Thanks. I've been stuck in my dorm working on a paper-finally finished it."

"Let me buy you a beer. You probably want to relax." With that, he began to massage my shoulders and neck.

"Oh wow, thanks for the neck rub, but I'm meeting someone else tonight."

"Cool," he answered. "I'll move on to greener pastures." It was that simple. I knew that soon the Rathskeller would be emptying out and, as much as I would have enjoyed a neck massage, I didn't want him to waste precious time on an unpromising prospect. There was a fertile field and we were all sampling its abundance.

In my social group in college, we told each other we didn't keep "numbers," even though it is fairly common for people to keep a mental list of partners they have had. I think we all secretly knew our numbers; I know mine. I hadn't thought about it for twenty-five years and would have been happy to bury the information for another twenty-five years until one day, when I was riding in the car with my twenty-year old daughter, the Z-100 radio morning crew began discussing people's "numbers." They reached a consensus that 4 to 5 partners was a desirable amount that established that a woman was neither a prude nor too loose. Interesting to note was the fact that lying about one's number was as frequent an occurrence as lying about one's age or weight.

When the morning crew finished their talk, my daughter chimed in and asked, "Mom, what was your number?"

"One that you will never know, my dear," was my only answer. I appreciated that she wanted to bond with me, woman to woman, but I decided to take that secret to my grave. I imagine it must be sentimental for someone who married a high school sweetheart and never slept around to know that sex has always been an expression of love towards one special person. For me, the early seventies was a time of experimentation on several levels, sex being only one of them.

As for the drugs of the seventies, the house that I lived in during college on Myrtle Avenue had your usual fare of ice cream in the freezer, but one housemate supported himself by selling blotter acid (a form of LSD), which he stored in our freezer. I was the den mother who cleaned up after a stoned friend spilled his or her beverage at dinner, although I cannot claim complete abstinence. It is miraculous that I survived all of the stupidity of my youth.

I was a foreign language major, which gave me the pretense for combining adventure with studying languages and cultures. I went on every foreign studies program the university had to offer. The American dollar was strong and it was less expensive to live abroad than to stay in the good ole U.S.A. This gave me the chance to exercise my lack of discretion on an international scope.

Let me preface the next episode by stating that none of my clients who has been arrested *ever* did anything illegal. When I ask what happened, whether it was a drug, weapon, or shoplifted item, the account invariably begins with "My friends ..." That being said, top on my list of poor discretion was that I was with *my friends* who were tripping on LSD when we were studying in Madrid, Spain. This was during the reign of the Dictator Franco when there were armed guards of the fascist Falange at every corner.

I was naive about the absolute authority of a despot. My passport disappeared from my pocketbook while I was taking a yoga class and the police called me up several days later to tell me I could retrieve it from the police station. There was no explanation given but I'm sure the government thought they had to investigate me, presumably thinking that yoga was a subversive activity and an American doing yoga made it even more so. Drug use in that police state environment was nothing short of insane.

My friends (high on LSD) and I locked arms and walked down the sidewalk beside a ten-lane avenue through the center of Madrid, across traffic circles and around picturesque fountains. At each intersection, we stopped at the corner and checked the traffic light. It had international signals; a red man standing still or a green man walking. We stayed alive by waiting to see the green man walking before crossing!

In those years, I felt invincible and took terrible risks hitch hiking and traveling alone. I found myself exiting a car and running down the middle of a road in Spain trying to flag down a passing car. I was pinned against a wall by a French cab driver after I exited his cab. I was set up to miss my flight from Ecuador by an airport employee who registered me in a nearby hotel as his wife. #MeToo.

These escapades and others served a very important purpose for me later in life when I listened to my own children's lapses in judgment without batting an eyelash. Naturally, I was very selective about how much I shared with them of my own indiscretions, like my "number."

Sex, drugs, and, oh yes, rock n'roll. Music was a sustaining staple, as vital as bread, before carbs fell into disfavor and gluten-free became a thing. While war was raging in Southeast Asia, a battle was underway at the State University at Albany over the student government's decision to spend the entire year's entertainment budget on one concert. The Allman Brothers Band was widely popular, but the tradeoff of having only one concert for the whole school year aroused the wrath of a number of normally complacent students. Perhaps the controversy was a welcome distraction from Napalm bombing of villages and death tolls on the evening news. Music, with its lyrical elixir, was the medicine for our confused souls.

Crosby, Stills, Nash and Young, Jethro Tull, Pink Floyd, the Allman Brothers Band, the Rolling Stones, and Eric Clapton were working towards becoming classic rockers. I read the book Long Time Gone by David Crosby that chronicles his experience from the sixties through the eighties. There's a saying that, if you remember the sixties and seventies, you weren't really there. In David Crosby's case, his recollections were so warped by drug use that his autobiography had to be balanced with objective fact checking by people who were around at the time. One anecdote from Long Time Gone that stands out is the image of David Crosby's girlfriend cooking pancakes wearing nothing but an apron.

Nudity was all the rage in the late sixties and early seventies. The Broadway musical Hair led the way with all of the actors disrobing on stage. I witnessed a streaker letting it all hang out running down the Main Street of an otherwise quaint town. One personal au natural experience was at a lakeside sauna owned by the university. We baked in the wood burning sauna, worked up a sweat, and then ran, sans clothing, into the welcomed chilly waters of the lake. I remember pointing to a group of students who had arrived wearing clothing and saying, "Look at those voyeurs."

Another favorite spot for nude sunbathing was the rooftop of a friend's house. In Albany, the students lived off campus in Victorian homes with turrets and wrap around porches. These beautiful examples of turn-of-the century architecture, once owned by distinguished families, were converted into multiple student dwellings that would make their original owners turn in their graves. For us, the advantage of this large several-story house where we were sunbathing was that a messenger was able to race up three flights of stairs to warn us that police were on their way after a spoil sport neighbor called to report us. We had enough time to throw on some clothing before the officer made it up the stairs. We greeted him with a polite, "Is there a problem, Officer?"

My stated university major was Spanish literature, but I minored in amorous liaisons in other countries. During those years before marriage and children, I lived my life as the proverbial rolling stone. We have all heard that a rolling stone gathers no moss. That is because moss has a complex manner of reproduction with sexual and asexual phases; a rolling stone never makes it to the asexual phase that is necessary to complete the reproductive cycle.

My first foreign studies were at the Goethe Institute in Germany where Fraulein Von Wrangle taught me German for six hours every day. She was six feet tall, wore a dirndl, smoked a cigar, and squeezed her large Bavarian frame into a Volkswagen bug. I was fresh out of high school and still a virgin so I didn't loosen any lederhosen. Instead, I spent a pastoral summer awakening to cowbells, hiking the foothills of the Alps, and drinking Bavarian beer at fests on the weekend.

When I attended a private university in Mexico City, I boarded with a Senora who insisted I adhere to the very strict rules of her household, including taking a chaperon with me when I went on a date. Her own daughters were spinsters. My first Mexican boyfriend was named Fernando Mercado, which I thought was an absolutely romantic sounding name until a friend pointed out that it translated to "Freddy Market" in English. Fernando was an artist who sketched my portrait and gave me gifts of his artwork. He was from a wealthy family and had lived in the United States for several years when he was in high school.

Somehow, Freddy and I managed to elude the Senora and the spinster daughters long enough to get away for a weekend. I lost my virginity at age nineteen to Freddy Market in a hotel in Acapulco. It seemed that my years from puberty on had built up to that moment and, I have to say about such inexperienced lovemaking, it passed without great fanfare. The loss of virginity is a momentous event. No matter what the actual experience, being a virgin or not being one is an identity and everyone remembers the situation. I invited a group of women to a feedback session. I asked each woman where, at what age, and under what circumstances she had lost her virginity.

My premise was that many of my peers had lost their virginity in the back seat of a car. Three out of seven did cite a car, though one was in the front. Presumably, there was no stick shift or bucket seats, and cars were much bigger back then. Two of the car stories involved a police officer's flashlight shining in on them, definitely a drawback to that setting. The feedback also confirmed that a hotel in Acapulco was not an ordinary venue. I continued to carry on my love life in unconventional settings.

The CIDOC Institute for cultural learning in Cuernavaca, Mexico provided more freedom in thought and lifestyle than living with the Senora, that is, if you don't count the brief stint I spent living in a dorm run by cloistered Carmelite nuns. The convent and I were not a good match. When the caretaker caught a male friend of mine slipping out of my room late one night, I knew it was time to pack my bags and leave ahead of my eviction notice.

The move from the convent was a trade up that brought me to a boarding house populated with American students and surrounded by beautiful gardens. I started each day doing yoga on a blanket spread in front of pink-flowering Bougainvillea and I came to fully appreciate why Cuernavaca was known as the City of Eternal Spring. It was a peak experience in my life. I met my second Mexican boy-friend at the boarding house in that romantic setting.

The hippie credo in those days was "back to nature" and Juan was the real thing: simple and earthy. When I was sick with allergies from the tropical flora, he gathered and boiled eucalyptus leaves to create a natural vaporizer for me. One of my favorite memories is of clinging tightly to his thin, muscular body as I rode on the back of his motorcycle, hair flowing in the wind. We crossed the open fields to arrive at a pyramid for a picnic lunch most likely of cheese and fruit because I had become a vegetarian.

Juan was not of the same social standing as Fernando. When I had a pregnancy scare, Juan planned a life for us in an adobe room adjoining his parents' house. When my parents came to visit me in Cuernavaca, they took us out to a fine restaurant. The waiter delayed serving us for an inordinate length of time, hoping we would get up and leave. We assumed they disapproved of my peasant-stock boy-friend, but it is just as possible that they may have disapproved of me since, by that point, I had gone native in my embroidered linen dress and unshaved armpits and legs. Either way, we were clearly undesirable patrons.

I grew up in a middle class environment with white-collar pro-fessional parents who raised my brother and me according to the guidance of baby doctor Benjamin Spock. His <u>Baby and Child Care</u> was their generation's parenting manual. The renowned pedi-atrician and author pointed out that, while in other cultures the parents were revered and held to be superior, we expect our children to take our accomplishments to the next level. The desire of parents from my parents' generation was to have their children exceed their achievements.

My parents envisioned a life for me that continued to build on their lives in terms of professional accomplishment and material success. A barefoot and pregnant life didn't meet these expectations. I had been well programmed by them and I left Juan behind to finish my final year of college. My Mexican liaisons were never intended to amount to anything permanent or confining. There was an element of safety in knowing, even if only on a subconscious level, that I was there for a few months and that an expiration date was attached to each romance. My parents weren't privy to this safety net concept and my adventures nearly drove them to their wits' end.

Years later, my brother reported that my parents had been fully prepared to kidnap me and stage an intervention. They were never vindictive people who said, "I hope your children give you as many sleepless nights as you have given us" or some other variation on that theme. I will say that, even without wishing that retribution on me, they lived to see proof when my children drove me to distraction, that what goes around comes around.

By my last semester abroad, in Spain, my parents were shell-shocked. I wrote to them about studying art in El Prado, visiting Roman aqueducts in Toledo, admiring the exquisite beauty of the Alhambra, and frequenting the tapas bars of Madrid. They kept waiting for me to drop a bomb and announce I had run off to live in a villa in Segovia, but ultimately, their fears that I had fallen off the Middle Class American track were unwarranted. I chalked up my dalliances to obtaining an up-close and personal understanding of the foreign cultures I was studying and came back to complete my degree at SUNY Albany.

On spring break before graduating college in 1973, my brother invited me to take a trip from the east to the west coast with him, his girlfriend, and her son in an old Volkswagen van. I accepted the offer. I was young and single and my "To-Do List" for the first half of the 1970's had check marks next to "sun-bathe nude," "sleep around," "*hang out with friends* who experimented with mind-altering drugs," "study in other countries," and "drive parents crazy." It was an open-ended list with room for a trip cross-country in a barely-running van.

We arrived in the Grand Canyon during a snowfall and couldn't see more than a foot in front of our faces. After weathering the night in the back of the van by piling sleeping bags on top of us, we awoke hoping to get a glimpse of the canyon only to leave disappointed. I may be one of the few who went to the Grand Canyon and didn't actually see it.

Making it to hippie Mecca, San Francisco, on a shoestring budget, we sought the cheapest hotel we could find. My brother and his girlfriend sent me ahead, while they parked, to get a room at a place that looked sufficiently cheesy to be within our price range. The hotel clerk had a very strange look on his face when I asked for twin beds for his girlfriend's son and me.

"You have a child with you?" he asked while he glanced nervously past me.

I turned around and looked into the eyes of an unamused pimp. He was a large man with a shaved head whose lap was occupied by a petite lady clad in a mini-skirt and platform shoes. The other women of the night were lounging around on couches and chairs. I eased myself out the door of the brothel and broke into a run. That night we slept in the van behind a gas station. There were so many breath-taking sights on that trip cross country, from the giant Saguaro cactus in the Arizona Sonora Desert to the majestic Redwoods in Muir Woods, that it was a memorable journey.

After graduating from college, I found a summer job in a community center on the North Shore of Long Island in Port Washington. My plan was simple, to work until I made enough money to continue seeing the world. When I had saved a few dollars, it was time to pick my next destination and I sought the most exotic place I could find. In the travel agency, I happened upon a brochure about the Galapagos Islands. These islands, owned by Ecuador on the Equator, were where Darwin developed his famous survival of the fittest theory. I booked a no-frills cruise on what I later learned was a converted icebreaker. Despite the need to begin each day with a dose of Dramamine, the setting was otherwise perfect for-what else-romance.

I now know from my present day perspective that there are two types of love. First, there is the kind of love that Leon Russell sang about in his tune "A Song For You." It is as close as I can come to a definition of the love one feels for a soul mate, a love that transcends space and time. The other type of love is pseudo-love that only functions in a specific setting. One friend's mother warned her daughter about the pseudo-love trap; the mother had met my friend's father in Rome. When the friend was planning to spend the summer in Italy during her college years, her mother said, "Remember, if you fall in love, you are falling in love with Italy, not the man."

The attraction that developed between a Costa Rican named Marco and me was of this pseudo-love type, intense but defined by time and space parameters. We had nothing in common other than the fact that we were both tourists exploring a fascinating place. Marco and I swam among seals in the Galapagos Islands in one of the most perfect moments up to that point of my life. He was strikingly handsome and the place was pristine. It was easy to forget the rest of the world as seals frolicked below me. Back on the mainland in Ecuador, we traveled by bus to the beginning of the Amazon River and picked bananas in the jungle as huge blue butterflies fluttered overhead.

It was a relationship that could only function in that paradise. The gift was a trip from his parents, and he was still entering skateboard competitions. I was, by this point, a college graduate, employed and living independently. After ten wonderful days, we parted with heavy hearts and headed home to our respective countries with no thought of ever seeing each other again.

On the airplane ride back to New York, I looked out the window at tufts of clouds that floated in the air between me and the expanse of ocean below. I remembered how I had sat alone one starlit night on the bow of the icebreaker watching it cleave the waves of the Pacific Ocean. I had felt the pangs of a cosmic loneliness and vowed never to be so far away from home again. For five years, I had sampled relationships like morsels from a smorgasbord. These fleeting relationships didn't satisfy the hunger for a person with whom I could share the rest of my life.

I had breathed the fragrant, moisture-laden air of the rain forest and the thin, crisp air of an Alpine mountaintop. I had wiggled my toes and floated in the Atlantic and Pacific oceans, but I felt adrift in the water. People talk about putting down roots, comparing their lives to that part of the plant that anchors it to the earth. Algae, fungi, and liverworts are plants that don't have roots. Since you are known by the company you keep, it was time to distance myself from the rootless genus and seek deeper attachments in terra firma.

My university major was Spanish literature but I minored
in amorous liaisons in other countries.

TWO

Disco Dropout

Meaningful relationships arise out of meaningful lives, but here's the million dollar question: how does one go about creating a meaningful life? I never daydreamed about marrying a good provider. My consciousness was raised enough to not want to place my future well-being dependent upon a man. My first priority needed to be a career. The community center where I found my summer job following graduation offered me a permanent position as a community counselor. The pay was barely enough to make ends meet but I thought it would help me find out if social work suited me. I moved into a house in Port Washington with a co-worker.

The small harbor village of Port Washington turned out to be a surprising Long Island secret. I had grown up in the mid-island area that featured blacktop, strip malls, and fast food chains. My new town had a different vibe. The community center was located across the street from the town dock and Louie's Shore Restaurant. It was enveloped by the aroma of garlic and seafood, the sound of clanking buoys floated in the air, and an armada of sailboats stood ready for an imaginary regatta. The charming community helped me transition into a more stable life.

My assignment at the Community Center was to work on a team with two men providing services and referrals to the clients who visited the center. There was a television show at the time called The Mod Squad with a politically correct trio made up of a black guy, a white guy, and a gal. My colleagues and I named ourselves "The Odd Squad." Our team was comprised of Tyrone, a six-foot-five black man, Chuck, a six foot four white-bread-and-mayo fellow with salt and pepper hair, and me, a short girl with freckles.

I met best-selling author and motivational speaker Dr. Wayne Dyer through counselor training sessions while I worked with the Odd Squad. When attention was focused on me in the training, I broke into tears. Not discreet tears, but embarrassing noisy sobs and wet cheeks. Wayne gave me an appointment for a private counseling session to explore the reason why I cried so easily. Overcoming that behavior would be an important lifelong lesson. He invited me to join a counseling group to work on feelings of vulnerability. The group was empowering and I remained in it for close to two years. During that time, Wayne and I bonded and I began to promote speaking engagements for him. We started small with an audience of one hundred people in the local school auditorium. The audience quickly doubled. After Wayne's first book, Erroneous Zones, was published, he bounded up the stairs of the community center where I worked to give me an inscribed copy.

Wayne was always a mischievous person. He used to tell the story of how he thought his teacher in elementary school had labeled him a disturbing elephant, only to realize years later that she was saying a disturbing *element*. The inscription he wrote in my book was pure Wayne. It played the same mind trick as the title of his book, which led your mind to read "Erogenous" until you took a second look. He wrote, "May this book tickle your uvula." He saw me process the words and frown. I thought I would have to clarify if I showed it to someone that "uvula" was the fleshy lobe in the back of a throat. Wayne ran back to his car and inscribed another book. This time he wrote, "I love you. Really I do. You are something special. 3/1/76." That's the book I still own. I don't know what became of the uvula book.

I believed, as the inscription said, that Wayne loved me, although I didn't know exactly in what way. He was very free with those words. He once asked me how I felt about him. I shrugged my shoulders and answered, "You are unattainable." "Unattainable?" he repeated as a question. End of conversation. What I meant was that how I felt about him was irrelevant because he was unattainable. Wayne was engaged to be married. We already had blurred lines of patient/therapist, mentor/mentee, and speaking engagement collaborators. There was one line I didn't want to cross. Today, as a more secure individual I might have answered, "I admire and love you."

Wayne asked if I would travel cross-country with him to set up speaking engagements as his personal assistant. My impetuous nature yielded to some thoughts of caution and the goal I had set to establish roots. What exactly was the job description of "personal assistant" traveling with a charismatic man twelve years my senior for whom I had strong feelings and who was engaged to be married? I decided that declining his offer would be the better part of valor. Besides, how could I give up my steady, though meager, wage for an unknown income?

Erroneous Zones went on to sell over 35 million copies with a sustained run on the New York Times best seller list. Wayne made the talk show rounds including several appearances on the Tonight Show with late night icon, Johnny Carson. From that point on, I saw Wayne only when he was speaking in New York, but his influence on me re-surfaced at critical times in my life, including in a most unusual way after his death forty-two years later.

I continued the work of the Odd Squad. One of my responsibilities was the administration of a bail bonds fund that exposed me to courtroom drama. The adrenaline rush of speaking to a judge on behalf of one of the center's clients was appealing at that stage in my life. I saw that I could tip the scales of justice in favor of my client and make a difference. It caused me to set my career compass on a path of law.

I had already been out of college for three years when I took the Law School Aptitude Test. My skills were not fresh. I completed the math section by answering "C" to every problem. Through some miracle of grace, I was accepted to study at St. John's University evening law program. I explained in my admissions essay that I spoke Spanish fluently and wanted to work with an underrepresented Hispanic population. I'm fairly certain that is what opened doors for me, not my math score.

The law school was located in Jamaica, Queens which, geographically is on Long Island but is one of the boroughs of New York City. I drove the route to St. John's University on automatic pilot five nights per week; first through the wooded suburbs of Nassau County and, then into the more densely populated urban streets of Queens, memorizing rules of law along the way.

Once I had a minor accident on my way to class. When I pulled over and talked to the driver of the other car, I was always honest to a fault and blurted out, "I only looked down for a second." Besides immediately realizing it was a stupid thing to say, it also occurred to me that I had committed a declaration against my interests, which was an exception to the hearsay rule of evidence and could be held against me in a court of law. At that moment, I became aware that I was on my way to becoming a lawyer. My next realization was disturbing; I had no female model for this role and it would be up to me to define it for myself.

Going to law school at night dominated my life for four years. After one year of trying unsuccessfully to balance work and school, I was forced to give up my job at the Community Center and focus on my studies. I poured over huge treatises and shook in my shoes when I was called upon to brief a case in the lecture hall in front of one hundred peers and one scary professor who was right out of The Paper Chase. The dean of the school had glaring eyes that made me think, no matter how hard I had studied, it wasn't enough. I had to practice the skills I had learned in my group counseling to keep from crying under that scrutiny, although I wanted to more than once. As Jimmy Dugan, played by Tom Hanks, famously told his all woman team in the movie A League of Their Own, there is no crying in the game of baseball and there is definitely no crying in the law. We can't play the Damsel in Distress card if we want to be taken seriously in any career.

I missed the Odd Squad but it was stimulating to be back in the academic community, meeting in study groups and pushing myself to my intellectual limit. I had a professor who managed to make the Uniform Commercial Code interesting and, at the end of the semester, surprised us all by bowing and saying, "I salute the spiritual light within you." It was actually possible to combine talk of Bills of Lading and securities collateral with a deeper purpose of life.

My spiritual light and intellect were stoked in law school, but I found time to kindle a relationship with a young man I met in Port Washington. I was no longer in a situation where any relationship I started had an automatic expiration date. My love interest deepened and I believed this was the meaningful relationship I was seeking. Relationships are like sharks that lack a gas bladder to keep them afloat; they will sink and die if they aren't constantly in motion. After two years, my boyfriend and I weren't moving towards a common goal of living together so it became clear that the relationship was on its way to Davy Jones' locker.

The break-up wasn't pretty; I lost ten pounds in one week after I learned that he had been continuously unfaithful to me. When I was dismissed from class early and made a surprise visit to his house, I found out that he had been meeting, on a regular basis while I was in school, with someone from his job at Publisher's Clearinghouse. I lost that Sweepstake!

Flash back to age twelve; I had my first boyfriend and my first heartbreak. The relationship took an entire summer to mature. This Don Juan came to my block every day on his bicycle and sat on it for safety most of the time. He fashioned a ring for me in arts and crafts at day camp. By the end of the summer, he finally built up the nerve to ask me to go to the movies with him one afternoon. He suggested that we could walk to the movie theater which required him to take the big step of leaving behind the security of his bicycle.

The expected time came and went, as did the time the movie was to begin. All these years later, I can still remember what I was wearing: my favorite blouse, red and white check with ruffles, and a new pair of white shorts. It turned out that his mother had punished him and made him stay in his room. In those days, children didn't have telephones in their rooms or cell phones; he was incommunicado. He couldn't sneak off as much as a text message. Even if he had been able to call, he probably would have been too embarrassed to tell me that his mother wouldn't let him go.

Not knowing the reason for being stood-up, I cried my eyes out from hurt and embarrassment. My mother said, "It may be the first disappointment, but it won't be the last." Was it supposed to be comforting to know that I could expect many other disillusions in my future? The words were classic maternal wisdom that came back to me at poignant moments such as the time of the Big Bang Break-up with my Sweepstakes Sweetie.

After the break-up, my best friend tried to help me through the hard times by taking me out to dance clubs. The Age of Aquarius was waning and we were on the cusp of <u>Saturday Night Fever</u>. The transition of hippie to Dancing Queen was not easy; I didn't walk the walk or talk the talk. For God's sake, I didn't even know the complete Zodiac or which signs complemented my Aquarius with Capricorn rising. In those meat markets, my girlfriend was filet mignon and I was a hamburger, even wearing my hottest bell-bottoms and tightest fitting Huckapoo polyester shirt. Once when I was driving to a club with her in the front passenger seat, a police officer stopped us.

"Good evening, Young Lady. Are you aware that your headlight is out?"

"I know, Officer, it just went out. I'll replace it tomorrow." He took his ticket book out of his back pocket and leaned into my car window to see who was in my passenger seat. He put the ticket book away.

"How about this, Young Lady; I won't give you a ticket because your friend is so cute." He winked at her as he said it and she flashed him an appreciative smile.

My filet mignon friend had a great success rate at attracting dance partners and being asked for her telephone number, but they would have fared better with this burger patty. All of their "Saturday

Night Fever" macho moves were lost on her; she had sworn off relationships with men after suffering through a divorce. In my quest for the knight in shining armor who would restore my faith in men, the disco scene offered slim pickin's. One very smooth dance partner, who I shall dub Sir Dancealot, almost had me setting up a date after several dances together. Then he decided to tell me his deepest secret right there on the dance floor: "Do you know that I was born with a tail?" While this may have been a good conversation opener with other gals, I excused myself after thanking him for an enjoyable evening doing the Hustle.

Perhaps I could have handled it better on a second or third date-it might even have been a "seventh-dater"-after we began revealing ourselves to one another in layers, peeled away during private moments, rather than having that information shouted to me over blaring music in the reflected light of a mirror ball. Sir Dancealot had invested a great deal of energy into the evening and seemed confused when I walked away. He was probably thinking he should have stuck with, "What's your sign?"

My disco girlfriend decided to throw a girls-night-out party where a psychic had been invited to entertain us with readings. Always the adventurous one, I volunteered to go first. I thought it was a lark to have my future read. The psychic took my hand and said, "You've just had a disappointment with love. It was nobody's fault; you couldn't communicate with each other." All of the blood drained from my face and I swallowed hard. She continued, "Don't fret. Within six months, you will meet someone whom you will want to marry, and when you see your ex-boyfriend, he won't matter to you anymore."

I thought the prediction was preposterous. How could I be over my previous relationship and already in love with someone else in six short months? Hadn't I collapsed on my bathroom floor sobbing about the shattering of my hopes and the betrayals? At the same time, I was not totally ready to dismiss the possibility that this psychic really did have insight into the future. I have always been intrigued by the paranormal and it offered me hope. It turned out to be the first psychic experience to influence the course of my life, but not the last.

If I was to believe the psychic, Mr. Right was out there waiting to be discovered. There were no dating websites back then. I agreed to try another more time-honored tack; blind dates with people whom friends thought would make a perfect match. These attempts usually had the exact opposite of the desired effect, only managing to accentuate the first date awkwardness. Going on these blind dates was like the difference between easing into a favorite slipper and forcing my foot into a shoe one size too small, trying to wear it during two hours of uncomfortable small talk. Nothing fit.

There was one young man whom I spoke with at length on the telephone. He had a dreamy voice and was a graduate student. I felt very optimistic when we arranged a date; he was probably the one who was going to fulfill the psychic's prophecy. With on-line dating, couples have an opportunity to size each other up with a photo and profile before they meet. Swipe left or right. We had no such advantage back then. When my date picked me up, I thought, if he was my knight in shining armor, he was going to have to keep his shining helmet visor down. My Spidey senses should have been triggered when nobody mentioned his physical attributes.

A study published in the science journal Evolution and Human Behavior found that men and women on blind dates make their judgments in three seconds or less. I gave the relationship far more than a three-second chance, in part because of the psychic's prediction that I was destined to meet the love of my life and I didn't want to overlook him. After several more dates, I realized that I couldn't force an attraction that was nonexistent, prophecy or not.

The well-intended matchmaking continued. Melanie, whom I have known since birth, invited me to her house to meet a man who worked at the school where she was substitute teaching. He was not in on the set-up. He had long strawberry blonde hair and a reddish beard. My first impression was, not bad at all. Sitting on a lounge chair in Melanie's backyard that summer day, I chatted with her friend, Nick, without any embarrassing silences. He was an intriguing person; a college wrestler who ate bean sprouts. When I was growing up, people were divided into two distinct camps: jocks and hippies, with very little intermingling. It was a time of extremes but Nick appeared to have bridged the gap between the two. I accepted an invitation to his Fourth of July barbecue.

An American flag flapped in the breeze on the flagpole in front of Nick's house. Fleetwood Mac was playing on the stereo and people were dancing in the living room. Chicken sizzled on the grill outside and a keg of beer sat in the shade of a birch tree. The backyard, planted with flower and vegetable gardens, was on a canal. Four well-fed cats sunned themselves on the railroad ties that sectioned off the gardens, basking in light reflected off the water. I danced and talked with the guests, some of whom were siblings, as I learned that Nick was the oldest of six.

That night, Nick and I went for a swim in the canal. His skin was tanned from fishing and gardening and his long locks were sun bleached. My chestnut brown hair cascaded in waves to my waist. I weighed a tad over one hundred pounds. Nick admired my bathing suit clad body when I dipped into the canal. It felt great to be appreciated, a feeling that had been missing for a while in my life.

We danced in his living room and, for the first time since my break-up, it felt good for a man to hold me. My better judgment told me to take it slowly, this was not just another infatuation. He was leaving the next day for Hawaii and promised to call me when he came back. The turn of events, from mourning the end of my last relationship to being excited by the potential of finding love again, seemed so magical that I ignored the fact that there was an oil slick on my bathing suit when I emerged from my swim in the canal.

Not only did I receive a call when Nick came back ten days later, but he brought me a gift of a coral necklace and earrings. What followed was an intense, passion-filled summer. He was also recovering from a painful break-up, being one year into a marital separation. We found a mutual need to love and be loved.

One of the bonds we shared was an appreciation of music. I was a Beatles generation teen. My diary from 1964 has an entry on February 7, "BEATLES in the U.S. They landed at J.F.K and the reception was fantastic." Every page thereafter has the name of a Beatle. I loved them all in turn. When you see those old clips of the Beatles at Shea Stadium, I was one of the hysterical girls in the stadium, and a friend in my group did actually faint in the aisle. From the moment Nick and I met, we began going to concerts together and constantly listening to music playing in the house and in our cars. We sent a picture of us in matching white cover-alls to our favorite radio station, WNEW, and ended up on their calendar's listener collage.

In those early months of our relationship, Nick and I took boat rides on his Mako fishing boat through the winding canals out to the Great South Bay. Fishing, clamming, and crabbing were all new to me, but I was willing to keep an open mind to experiencing them. Standing knee deep in water, finding clams buried in the sand with my feet had an immediate gratification when we fired up the grill and made clams on the half shell to eat.

We were working off the high energy of love. This is a documented chemical state in which serotonin levels of the love-obsessed are equal to those suffering from excessive-compulsive disorder. Staying up all night making love or talking are made possible by this love-induced chemistry. One night in late August, we went out after dark on the boat and came back a little chilled. Nick made tea with rum, my first taste of a hot toddy. We sat on the floor of the hallway in his house drinking our hot toddies and talking until dawn.

Among all of the conversations and time we spent together, I can pinpoint that night as the moment when I knew that the relationship was right. We were listening to Joni Mitchell singing the song "Woodstock" and I commented on her beautiful description of bomber planes turning into butterflies.

"Bombers into butterflies; very cool way to talk about wanting peace. I was an alternate to go to college at West Point, so I wasn't anti-army, but I was against the Vietnam War, for sure."

"Were you in danger of being drafted?"

"No, I went into teaching right after college so I could stay one step ahead of the draft board. I was twenty-one and hardly knew what I wanted to do with my life but I certainly knew what I didn't want to do."

"You know, I read that Joni Mitchell didn't actually go to Woodstock but wrote the song after her friends Crosby, Stills and Nash told her about it. I had tickets," I said, proud of that fact, "but they closed the New York State Thruway. I couldn't get off Long Island."

"I was there," Nick said. "Yeah, I drove up to Sullivan County with two gals who lived on my block. My brother Jim said he was going to meet us up there, but I realized when we arrived into the sea of people that it was going to be impossible to find him. Then, in the midst of one million people, Jim walked up to me as if he had bumped into me at the corner store, and asked if I wanted to go skinny dipping with some cool people he had met."

One great story ran into another and I realized that Nick was a hippie kindred spirit who saw eye to eye with me on politics, religion, and pop culture. When I met him, I still had two years of law school ahead of me, but he was not intimidated, as I had found some men to be when I spoke about a career in law. This was the 1970's and a male classmate told me he could never marry a woman lawyer. Nick, on the other hand, welcomed my career ambitions.

The psychic's words came back to me: "Within six months, you will meet someone whom you will want to marry . . ." I was as embedded as a deep taproot seeking a water table and, within six months, moved into Nick's house in Bellmore on Long Island. After living in Germany, Spain, and Mexico, sailing over the equator in an icebreaker, and driving cross-country in a van by the time I was twenty-one, I came back to roost on Long Island less than ten miles from where I grew up. Having experienced love on a variety of latitudes and longitudes, I ended up in a relationship with a homegrown guy.

It reminded me of the musical, The Fantasticks. The enduring theme of that show is that the girl and boy next door travel around the world separately seeking adventure and discover that their fulfilment was with each other right in their own backyards.

After I saw the play <u>The Fantasticks</u> with my parents, my father said, "You see, everything you want is in your own backyard if you only open your eyes to see it."

I answered, "How can you ever know that what you have is what you want if you haven't looked around first?"

I still stand by my interpretation. You can quickly recover from the regret of doing something that didn't work out well for you, but the regret that lingers a lifetime is that of not having done things you longed to do or not knowing what else might have been out there. I believed I had looked around enough to know that Nick was the person I was supposed to find.

There was a second part to the psychic's prediction: "When you see your ex-boyfriend, he won't matter to you anymore." After being with Nick for eight or nine months, I called my ex to put closure on the terrible break-up. I wanted to say that I was getting on with my life and I was probably just a little interested in finding out how I would feel seeing him. We went out to lunch. I sat across the table from him picking at my salad and thinking it strange that I felt no physical attraction to him.

"What made you call after all this time?" he asked.

"We left things on such a bad note. I thought a two-year relationship deserved a better ending."

"Maybe it doesn't have to be an ending," he suggested.

"Oh, yes, it does," I answered.

"No second chances?"

"No, but thanks for considering it." I thought to myself that I had found my new Sweepstake.

On my second Fourth of July with Nick, I was overcome with the fullness that I felt from the warm, friendly people he had drawn to him. A gathering of his family alone created a happening. I came from a quiet family with one sibling and had one good friend who had been like a sister when we were growing up. When my brother left for college and my girlfriend and I drifted apart in high school, I felt very solitary. Although I had learned to be a self-reliant person, traveling thousands of miles by myself, I knew loneliness. I enjoyed the notion that I would never be alone if I stayed with Nick, who was a "people person."

In the 1971 movie Harold and Maude, a young boy obsessed with death learns to love life from a seventy-something woman who has a joy of living. Harold comments that Maude is so good with people and she explains, matter-of-factly, that it's because they are the same species. If only it were that simple. I have never found it to be easy. Nick was good at relating to his species and I valued that trait.

By the end of 1979, I had traversed a decade spanning the diametric extremes of counter cultural experimentation and mind numbing disco. Improbably, I emerged with my love life and career path on a navigable course towards a committed relationship and a profession. By any definition, I had put down roots and was headed towards a meaningful life with a meaningful relationship. My "to-do" list 1975-1980 had large check marks next to "find career," "find mate," and "put Mexican embroidered peasant dress into cedar chest for storage."

His skin was tanned from fishing and gardening
and his long locks were sun bleached.

THREE

Pepto-Bismol in the Wedding Photo

In one of a long series of contradictions in my relationship with Nick, I decided on Independence Day to give up my independence and marry a person I thought would make a suitable life mate. Author J. Bronowski, in <u>The Ascent of Man</u>, observes that sex was invented by green algae. But as people, we are very particular about with whom we beget children. Choosing an appropriate mate insures survival of the fittest, a theory I had learned all about in the Galapagos Islands. I would not choose to marry someone born with a tail, even if a very good dancer. That's just not the direction I want my species to go. Nick, on the other hand, was a person I could see myself begetting with and I hoped our union would prove as favorable to our species as the natural selection process had for the Galapagos Blue-Footed Boobie.

It never crossed my mind that Nick might not want to marry me, and maybe I was wrong to assume, but I informed him that I wanted to marry him. Shy and demure, traits associated with femininity, were never adjectives used to describe me. It probably would have been nicer if there had been a romantic proposal, especially when years later the product of our union, one of our "begets," asked me, "How did Daddy propose to you?" My daughter was jumping on my bed while I put away laundry.

"Well, honey, I actually asked him."

"I thought the man is supposed to ask the woman to marry him," she said, doing a knee drop to the mattress and springing back up

"Many times it happens that way, but my mother asked my father to marry her also."

"Grandma asked Grandpa to marry her?"

"Yes, she did. He was in the army during World War II and they were going to transfer him to another state. She was afraid she might never see him again and her heart was breaking."

"Was his heart breaking also?"

"It was, but he thought it would be selfish to ask her to marry him because he was being shipped away and didn't know if he would be sent to battle and maybe die."

"Wasn't she afraid to marry him and then be a widow?'

"She told him she didn't care if she was married to him for only one hour and she would follow him anywhere."

"Wow!" Rhea stopped her jumping. "Maybe when I grow up I'll ask my boyfriend to marry me."

Proposals come in all sizes and shapes. My nephew planned how he would pop the question for weeks. He brought his beloved to the place where they had their first date and presented her with the engagement ring of her dreams. Then there is the approach taken by one friend's husband who tried to low-key his proposal. He was out for a stroll with his love and they passed a jewelry store. He pointed to a wedding band and said, "I don't suppose you would want one of those." Responding in kind she said, "Yeah, why not." There was a minimum amount of risk involved for both in the proposal and response.

Once the die was cast for Nick and me, I had a slight case of cold feet. Nick was a very complex person, alternately gregarious and fun but quick to anger. The bean sprout part of him wanted peace in the world and a garden with cats lying in it, but the wrestler in him was combative. We were both very stubborn and locked horns on a regular basis. I began to go to therapy and complain about everything that was wrong with him. My therapist looked up from her note pad, pushed her bifocals to the end of her nose and gazed at me over them.

"So let me understand this, Linda. You are coming to therapy because Nick needs help?"

"When you put it that way, I guess I have to deal with my own problems. But, really, my biggest problem is that he is so difficult and challenging!"

There was one very messy detail that was not psychological-Nick was still married to his first wife, though they were legally separated. There were no children from their marriage. There was, however, a lengthy section in their separation agreement awarding Nick custody of their cats with liberal visitation privileges for his wife. I was working at a law firm while going to law school and I was able to solicit the help of one of the lawyers to complete the conversion of the separation into a legal divorce. I drafted the paperwork myself and made arrangements directly with his ex-wife for service of process on her.

I liked his ex a great deal but harbored just a small amount of jealousy that didn't truly end until years later when I reached what to me was a milestone; being married more years to Nick than she had been. The ex came over to the house, we drank wine, she signed papers, and I notarized them. Before leaving, she managed to take back a few miscellaneous items of marital property that she determined were rightfully hers.

This may not come as a surprise, but the clerk of the divorce court detected that there might have been some irregularity in the paperwork. Maybe it was the fact that, after several glasses of wine, I had affixed my notary stamp upside down. Nick was called in for an inquest to answer a few questions, and I had to take the stand to explain how I had served his wife with the Summons and Complaint. All questions being satisfactorily answered, the divorce was finalized.

I have characterized the first marriage as a "messy detail" in our relationship, but I didn't view it entirely as a negative. Since a child, I had an irrational fear of my husband divorcing me. My instincts told me that, because Nick had been married before, he was not likely to divorce again. I didn't know whether the statistics bore that out, however, the way I saw it, Nick had already experienced the pitfalls of marriage, and maybe had acquired some skills to avoid them in the future. I also thought he would not be anxious to be that person who was divorced twice. There would be a degree of security in being wife number two.

Nick and I were free to make public our plans to wed. A date needed to be set, and since I was still in law school, our wedding had to be either the year before the Bar Exam or the year after, because the Bar Exam needed my undivided attention. Nick noted that our wedding was playing second fiddle to a licensing exam.

I waived getting an engagement ring and saved on the cost of wedding rings by buying them at Consumer Distributors. My morning radio show posed the question to its listeners of what extreme measures people had taken in order to purchase extravagant engagement rings. Several callers recounted selling cars to finance diamond engagement rings. I know of one young lady who took a loan to pay for a conversation-stopping engagement ring and a wedding at a fancy country club. The only problem was that she was divorced before the loan was repaid.

These acts of excess never made sense to me. Our friend, Charlie, would explain it by his theory that the bigger the wedding, the sooner the divorce. He says he has tracked his theory for many years with surprising accuracy. The hypothesis behind the theory, he says, is that people make up for inadequacies in their relationship by focusing their attention on the accoutrements of the wedding. According to the Charlie theory, I must have felt very secure in our relationship since I gave such superficial attention to our wedding.

When the staff at the junior high where Nick taught gave us an engagement party at the school, I showed up in jeans and a t-shirt. They gave us a gift of elegant champagne flutes. One of the teachers made the off-handed comment, "Nice of you to come so dressed up."

I answered, "The party is a stop on my way to school this evening." That proved to be a metaphor for the wedding, even if not for the marriage. We had been living together for over a year so the nuptials were a formality to me. Once I made the commitment to live with him, I no longer considered myself single.

I was very vocal on the issue of not wanting Nick to have a bachelor's party. I argued that he wasn't a bachelor since we were already cohabiting and sharing our lives on so many levels. I also strongly objected to the idea that I would be expected to pose for pictures with a bonnet of bows balanced on my head at a wedding shower while Nick would be balancing a stripper on his lap at a bachelor's party.

Women's liberation had not eroded these firmly entrenched sexist rites of passage when I was a bride-to-be. Today, progress has brought us to a new level of awareness; women have bachelorette parties that are every bit as bawdy as their male counterpart's. Strippers are routine entertainment at these parties, and Grandma and Great Auntie usually are not invited guests. Gift and novelty stores carry a line of favors for these events such as a button saying "Buy me a shot, I'm tying the knot." At one party, the gals went around the table sharing their answer to the question, "How many dates did you have before getting down to business with your significant other?"

While I don't agree with the principle of a party dedicated to having one last fling before committing to the anticipated tyranny of marriage, I think it is some progress that women and men participate equally in the pre-nuptial festivities and I welcome any opportunity for female bonding. A good friend of ours who was privy to my stag party debate came to the rescue by surprising Nick and me with a bachelor/bachelorette party in her home attended by several couples. That solved the bachelor party issue but there were far greater challenges to be faced.

For the wedding ceremony, Nick and I envisioned a small gathering of friends and family for cake and champagne at our church. My parents pushed for a more elaborate event. They were uncomfortable with a wedding in a Church presided over by a minister. I was raised in a Jewish household. We observed the holidays and went to synagogue on the High Holy days. My brother went to Hebrew School and had a Bar Mitzvah, but my parents decided not to send me for religious education because it wasn't as important, in their opinion, for a girl to have a Bat Mitzvah. It seemed a little hypocritical to see my parents dig their heels in on the religious issue since they had never pushed religion with me up to that point.

The other curious fact was that my mother had converted to Judaism. When she met my father, he was teaching radar to soldiers at Vanderbilt University. His fraternity brother, Lou, had passed along his little black book before being shipped out of Nashville and that book led my father to his future bride. My dad came from an Orthodox Jewish home in the tenements of Brooklyn and my mom from a farm on Ben Allen Road in the outskirts of Nashville. There is not much good you can say about any war but one silver lining to World War II was that it opened up the world to so many who had lived very provincial lives up to that point, and helped to form life-long bonds between people.

My mother was Protestant and had never met a Jewish person before. My father was a swarthy, ethnic looking man with a large nose and enough body hair on his torso to make a mohair sweater. She was fair skinned, with strong but well proportioned features and her fine red hair was worn in the upswept style of the forties. His New York Jewish accent was as strong as her Southern drawl. It was a veritable culture collision.

My mother thought she had found some common ground between her family and my father, in that her cousin David Hugh was a scientist like my father. She arranged a meeting. David was an Oak Ridge nuclear physicist who decided he didn't care too much for that kind of work and went back to dairy farming. He invited my father to follow him around the farm while he did some chores. David never looked down but nevertheless managed to miss all of the cow droppings, while Brooklyn Jackie, as he was known in the army, kept his eyes glued to the ground and stepped in almost every pile. Back at the farmhouse, David poured his coffee into the saucer, blew on it to cool it down and slurped it from the saucer without a trace of inhibition. My father's eyes were as wide as that saucer.

Despite the improbability of the match between my mother and father, the marriage lasted over sixty years. It was one of those loves I described that transcends space and time. My maternal grandmother sweetly accepted my mother's conversion to Judaism. While Judaism was very foreign to her, she rationalized that it was expected for her daughter to take the religion of her husband. My father's mother embraced her new daughter-in-law, saying in her Yiddish accent, "This is your home", the universal "Mi casa es tu casa." Privately, it must have been exceedingly difficult for each of my grandmothers to accept this inter-faith marriage, but World War II turned the world upside down and shook convention out of its pockets.

I followed my mother's actions, if not her words, and joined my husband's religion, the Unitarian Universalists. The Universalists believe in universal salvation, which was very appealing to me since I didn't relish the belief that I might burn for eternity in Hell for all of my transgressions. Purgatory was not much more inviting and the Catholic Church has not decided the future of the religious status of Limbo. Considering these options for eternity, I felt safer with my newly found liberal religion. Nick and I agreed that a minister would marry us.

We went to the Town Hall to apply for our marriage license. In the entranceway there was a directory with a list of activities that required licensing, including marriage and games of chance. What really gave me misgivings was the fact that the same Town Clerk's office issued licenses for dog ownership and marriage. A resident could conceivably register his or her dog and spouse on the same day. We applied for our license to wed.

Because I was going along with my parents' wedding reception idea and not mine, I made plans reluctantly. I chose a caterer who was starting a major renovation, and consequently, was offering a very large discount. I had to take it on faith that the renovation would be completed before my wedding. Predictably, my guests had to walk under a scaffold to enter the building and only the cocktail room had been refurbished. I'm sure that if I had subscribed to "Bride" magazine, I would never have made that mistake.

Melanie, who introduced Nick and me, was getting married around the same time. She had painstakingly planned every minuscule detail of her celebration. She and her husband, her parents, and her in-laws took dance lessons before the wedding. There would be no missteps when they joined the circle to do the Hora or Misirlou at her reception! Luckily, I was not competing for the better wedding because I had no shot at winning. Even so, I thought it was trivial when Melanie commented on how low the ceiling was in the banquet dining room. Later, when I tossed the bouquet over my head to the waiting single gals, the bouquet hit the exceedingly low ceiling and fell straight to the floor, several feet ahead of the group. I could always trust Melanie's honesty.

Those in the know told me that I was supposed to stay in the bridal suite during the cocktail hour so that nobody would see me before the ceremony. As far as I was concerned, I had never received that memo. My wedding dress was actually a bridesmaid gown with handkerchief points at the hem. I decided to remove the outer lace blouson from my gown and mingle with the guests in the strapless cocktail dress that was underneath the frills. When it came time for the ceremony, I donned the blouson and veil and emerged as superbride for the wedding ceremony.

In addition to compromising on the locale of the wedding, Nick and I gave in to my parents' request to have both a minister and a rabbi conduct the ceremony. I found a rabbi, through listings in the Yellow Pages, who was willing to share the stage with a minister. We were surprised when our hired gun clergyman turned up wearing a priest's collar at another wedding six months later! Nick and I began our married lives with the blessings of a Unitarian Minister and Rabbi "Have Yarmulke, Will Travel."

Looking back at the photos from the wedding, Nick and I appear very happy. One picture of me in the bridal suite before the ceremony told another side of the story; there were bottles of Tylenol and Pepto-Bismol on the table next to my bouquet. In case you are reading this book from somewhere in the outback, Pepto-Bismol is the only leading medicine that relieves five stomach conditions: heartburn, diarrhea, nausea, indigestion, and upset stomach, and I regret that I can't recite those to the tune of the commercial jingle.

The money we saved on rings was put towards a honeymoon in Greece. It was to be a ten-day tour with an island cruise. My suitcase was carefully packed to include every anticipated circumstance. A separate bag was dedicated to a shoe for every situation including sandals, sneakers, hiking boots, and high heels. I couldn't understand why Nick wasn't packing, even as a car was on its way to chauffeur us to the airport.

I was still clinging to my feminist fantasies that I would never pack for my husband, a competent adult and equal. As time slipped by without any indication of his suitcase being taken out of the closet, I had to take deep breaths and repeat the mantra, "He is a grown man…He is a grown man." The grown man was dancing around in his underwear while I went over my checklist of items to make sure I had packed everything I needed. This brings to mind a study of sexual differences in the learned behavior of chimps. While the female chimps practiced fishing for termites, the males spun themselves in circles. It was explained that this male behavior was not useless but rather served as practice for later dominance behavior.

Nick's underwear dancing also had a purpose. I feel bad, in retrospect, that I didn't pick up the clear call for help. I now recognize that it was the same behavior my father used to exhibit when he had to choose clothing to wear to a special occasion. He would not directly ask for help. It was that whole macho I-don't-need-to-ask-for-directions thing. My father would walk into the living room, where we were sitting, while buttoning his shirt. If we didn't like what he was putting on, we would say, "No, Dad, not that shirt!" and he would go back to his closet and come out buttoning another one. This process could be repeated several times before the final outfit was in place. He would never directly ask what he should wear. Likewise, Nick couldn't bring himself to ask me what he should pack but was hoping for me to rescue him. I fumbled and dropped the ball.

When we arrived at the hotel in Athens, I unpacked my large valise filled with outfits for dining out, touring, and going to the beach. Nick had a few items that he had thrown together: a pair of dirty shorts, a dirty t-shirt, a bathing suit, a button-down shirt, one pair of long pants, underwear, and socks. He boasted that it all fit into one carry-on case. I saw my feminist values slipping down the drain of the hotel room sink as I hand-washed the dirty shorts and t-shirt and hung them up to dry.

I thought of this years later, when I saw Defending the Caveman on Broadway. There is a scene in the beginning of a man and a woman getting ready to go out. The woman is primping and obsessing over the details of her outfit. The man reaches into the hamper, pulls out a shirt, sniffs it, and decides to put it on. If I had seen that show before our honeymoon, I would have known to help Nick with his packing.

There were so many memorable moments in Greece: at the ancient ruins, following the hairpin curves to Olympia, outdoor cafes, and, of course, the cruise to the Greek Isles. I'm not a great sea-faring traveler and spent most of the time on the ship in a state of seasickness. This culminated on the night of the Captain's dinner when there were white caps on the Aegean Sea. I was managing reasonably well with the courses until they served dessert: Flaming Cherries Jubilee. I staggered towards the door, without assistance from Nick who was fixated on his plate. A waiter came to my aid and helped me out, eager to avoid any unpleasantness in the dining room.

When I glimpsed back from the doorway, I saw Nick pulling my Cherries Jubilee in front of him. He spilled some on his one button-down shirt. I foresaw myself washing it out in the sink when he joined me back in our cabin later that evening. My marriage to Nick had been written in the stars, but Fate failed to mention that my husband would be oblivious to basic acceptable norms of grooming and manners.

The honeymoon was as good a time as any to establish ground rules for living with Nick. First, I learned that cherries jubilee prevails over chivalry. Secondly, I vowed never to let Nick pack for another trip. Call it rationalization, but I reconciled that this vow wasn't an abandonment of my feminist ideals, but rather recognition of our respective strengths and weaknesses. I rummaged through my bags, found my Pepto-Bismol, and took a generous dose. Items checked on my "To-do List" for 1978-79 included: "Propose marriage," "Plan tacky wedding," "Adjust relationship expectations."

There were bottles of Tylenol and Pepto-Bismol
on the table next to my bouquet.

FOUR

The Compost Bin on Farmers Avenue

Vows said and newly wed, I took a critical look around the house that was to be my marital residence. It was one thing being a live-in girlfriend, but a completely different perspective to now think of it as the home that would be a reflection of me, the woman of the house. Nick had bought the house with his first wife while still in his early twenties and put his heart and soul into personalizing it. He told me that he wanted to be buried in the backyard. It was his castle. The green canal separating our property from our neighbor's, at low tide, resembled a moat.

I recall one summer, when I was about ten years old, that I entertained myself by planning my future life. I cut out pictures from magazines of my future husband and my future home. My husband was going to be Michael Landon from Bonanza. My future home was going to be an old colonial with a wrap-around porch and perhaps a bit of Victorian bric-a-brac. It would be furnished in Danish modern furniture. Enter reality. I didn't marry Michael Landon, my house was a 1950-something Cape Cod with vinyl siding, and my marital home was furnished with wicker and antiques in various degrees of disrepair.

Our house was located on a dead end, literally and also metaphorically, since Nick never planned to leave. The street was a peninsula, surrounded on three sides by water, and when the tides, moon, and weather conspired against us, we had water in the street as well. I was still in law school and in no position to think about moving to another house so I did what I could with what I had.

Certain aspects of my new home required emergency attention. In the kitchen, on top of the cabinets, there was a very impressive, but dusty, beer bottle collection. I practiced how to tactfully suggest that it might be better stored away and, eventually, I put them in a box in the garage. They may still be there today and there may be a beer aficionado out there trolling on EBay who would be enthusiastic about acquiring this collection.

Next was the challenge of the fish tank in every room, all of which had green algae on the glass. I used to eat with my back towards the one in the kitchen so that I didn't have to watch the latest casualty floating sideways near the top. As the fish died off, I retired each tank. I'm actually quite an animal lover, but I am averse to uncared for aquariums with fish suffering from Ich and Tail Rot.

I acquired the four step-cats that were the subject of the custody agreement in his separation papers. I loved my step-cats like my own. They were named Jonathan, Jennifer, Stephanie, and Claudia. I became concerned that when we had children, Nick might lobby to name them Whiskers and Boots, but he reassured me that he would agree to appropriate names for our offspring. Owning four cats meant making accommodations for cat bowls, cat beds, cat toys, and kitty litter pans. I adapted.

The ex-wife considered herself an artist and enjoyed bold color. I had to address the color schemes in the house. When entering it, one could stand in the living room decorated with navy and red seat cushions, and look past the forest green hallway into the purple bathroom. I'm more of a taupe person. When I repainted the bathroom a pale, wheat color, I kept checking to see if the light had been left on because it was so much brighter. Then there was the subject of the ex's artwork. It was better than paint by number but still a work in progress.

"I got a call from my ex today," Nick said.

"What did she want?"

"She asked if she can come pick up her paintings. We already divided everything and she left the paintings because I didn't have anything to replace them."

"That's all right, honey. I know it's disappointing, but you should choose your battles. Don't fight her to keep them." I left the room to do my happy dance.

The year that Nick lived alone in the house after splitting with his first wife gave ample time to develop systemic dirt requiring a major cleaning campaign. I discovered that the banister, which I thought was antique white with golden streaks on it, was actually only dirty. When I passed a damp sponge over it, all of the "antiquing" washed away. Likewise, it turned out that a cement floor in the furnace room was really a sheet of brightly patterned linoleum covered with a layer of dirt.

The house had some charming qualities, especially the oak antiques, even if some needed repair. Most of my future furniture would be purchased in an antique store. There was a tiny den with a potbelly stove, which warmed the whole house and gave off a rich, rustic wood-burning scent. The kitchen featured a center island butcher-block that dominated the small kitchen so much that the center island felt like a center continent. We had countless fantastic times sitting on the barstools around that table, drinking beer and wine, and eating clams.

I was convinced, at that table, to try eel that a neighbor had smoked. This was before mainstream America had ever heard of sushi. My only previous association with eel was when a group of boys chased my best friend and me around our block with an eel on Halloween, when I was ten or eleven. When we did some much-needed renovations to the kitchen years later and took the butcher-block out to make the room more spacious, I cried.

Because we were located on the water, our house had no basement. It didn't have an attic. Storage space was a premium and we have always suffered from clutter. I'm no scientist, but I swore that things in our house propagated spontaneously. I wanted to try an experiment of hermetically sealing the drawer of plastic containers and covers, opening it a year later to see how it had multiplied. After hosting a party, I wanted to divide up leftovers for people to take home. My brother's wife just shook her head when I tried to open a drawer jammed full of plastic covers that no longer had matching containers (another phenomenon I would like to study; where did the bottoms go?) She said, "Linda, I think it's time to cull."

Culling is a good idea but it requires making administrative decisions: keep, toss, recycle, or give to the Thrift Shop. There is "stuff" that you will never use again that is impossible to part with because to do so acknowledges that you will not revisit that stage. I have a pocketbook graveyard on the top shelf of my closet. How can I dispose of a favorite hand-tooled leather bag from Mexico in the garbage if it is too worn for Thrift Shop recycling?

47

My mother used to have a baby stroller hanging up in our garage, until we were teenagers. She was superstitious that if she gave it away, she might get pregnant. I wanted to tell her that if the stroller hanging in the garage was her only form of birth control, she was at a high risk. We addressed our storage problem by putting a loft in the garage to store some of the things that we couldn't bear to lose.

Our house is appropriately located on Farmers Avenue. If the house was Nick's castle, the grounds were his estate. He only had a sixty-by-one-hundred area to work with so he created square foot gardens and managed to grow enough vegetables to freeze for the winter. Potted plants summered outdoors and wintered inside our house. We had a small fruit garden of pear trees, blueberry bushes, and a strawberry patch. There was no room on the estate for grass. In fact, our front yard didn't have a lawn, only gardens. Nick grew up on an acre of land and swore to never mow another lawn.

As newlyweds, couples need to adjust to idiosyncrasies if they want the relationship to work. My husband was an advocate of composting and maintained a pile to decompose organic garbage into rich soil for spreading over his gardens. Knowing how important composting was to him, I agreed to keep a compost container in the kitchen for disposing of organic garbage. Besides, my parents were gardeners and environmentalists so the idea of compost was familiar to me.

I put up with containers on the kitchen counter until we purchased state-of-the art compost buckets with charcoal filters to go under the sink. When Nick forgot to dig a hole in the ground before winter set in, freezing the earth, I wondered what he was doing with the compost buckets until one day I found them lined up in the garage. He said it was all right because it was so cold in the garage that it wouldn't become a nuisance. I wasn't convinced so we introduced another innovation to the composting process; an above ground, outdoor bin where we could dump our vegetable scraps into, year round. I was definitely complicit.

Sometimes I thought, or you might say dreamt, about moving to a more upscale block but I knew in my heart that we could never escape from Farmers Avenue. I could just see the reaction of new neighbors watching us unloading our large outdoor compost bin from the moving van. Nobody on this street blinks at Nick's activities. Before I arrived on the scene, they had lived through corn and pumpkin patches in the front yard. The side yard contains a stand of bamboo that could feed a Panda for a year. All of this lush growth was made possible through the miracle of composting.

Since environmentally conscious parents raised me, I was prepared for composting but I still found it odd that Nick stored praying mantis cocoons over winter in our garage refrigerator to be released into the gardens for pest control in the summer. I lived with fear that a guest might go into the garage to get a beer and pop one of these interesting morsels from the door shelf into his or her mouth, then, walk back asking, "What are these crunchy treats?" One woman I know told me that I shouldn't complain because her husband stores frozen lab mice in the freezer to feed to his pet snake. Commiseration can be so comforting; we can put up a cot in the misery-loves-company guestroom.

There seemed to be a limitless number of battles to undertake in marriage. I truly experienced first-hand the premise set forth by John Gray that men are from Mars and women are from Venus. Sometimes, I actually believe we are from different solar systems. I found it was helpful to understand each other's goals when we appeared to be working at odds with one another. One evening we were preparing to have guests over for dinner and I was racing around trying to clean up the kitchen.

"Nick, I just cleaned up over there. Why are you putting a chopping block out?"

"I want our guests to see me cooking." I didn't know I was living with Emeril Lagasse.

"I was hoping I could sit down with a glass of wine and greet them with a clean kitchen and all of the cooking done." Once we realized that we were working at cross-purposes, it was easier to arrive at a common ground; you put your chopping board there and I'll clean up around you.

All of the arguments were not as easily resolved when you are trying to make a house a home, when coming from vastly different perspectives. Once, I had worked all morning on cleaning up the furnace room, even going behind the furnace where no being except the cats had ever set foot. I left the house after this awful clean-up job to do some shopping and came home to a bad vibe so heavy it was tangible. When I saw Nick, he was distraught that I had thrown out a hanger found on the floor of the furnace room.

"Why are you so upset?" I asked him. "I thought it was just an old, bent hanger gathering cat fur and dust."

"It was an extra strong hanger and I had it bent perfectly to hang my fishing boots on so they could dry in the furnace room."

"We can find another heavy duty hanger and bend it in the same shape. I don't see why you are making such a big deal. And I also don't appreciate the fact that you aren't acknowledging the job I did cleaning up that damn mess in there."

"The mess was bothering you, not me. I don't want you throwing out anything of mine without asking. My father used to go on rampages and throw out my things. You wouldn't believe some of the stuff he threw out: airplane models that I spent days working on, baseball cards that would have been worth thousands of dollars today . . ."

"So that's what it's about."

These are the kinds of tearful fights that newlyweds are bound to encounter during the "getting to know you" stage. With all of the information I have today, I would have understood that disregard for his belongings was interpreted as disregard for him. I learned the hard way to be more aware of this sensitivity when I straightened up.

Another perspective that helped me deal with the challenges of our relationship was when I realized that I wanted to pick a fight on a regular monthly basis. It dawned on me that maybe this was linked with my biological cycle. It became apparent that it was my inability to let irritations roll off my back at those times that was leading to some of our blow ups. It's that PMS water retention thing, accompanied by the bloating and followed by bleeding that affects one's desire to be pleasant.

I began to tell myself "It's your period talking." If an issue still bothered me after my period, then I knew it was worth discussing. To be worth a fight, an issue had to meet the post-menstrual test: did his aggravating action seem as bad the week after I menstruated as it had the week before? While some people count to ten to calm down, I adopted the count to ten days method that went a long way to promote peace in our household.

We talked about having a family and set our goals on expanding the house to accommodate children. One important need was to create a laundry area for all that soiled kids' clothing we anticipated. When I first moved in, I took the laundry to a Laundromat.

Two of my sisters-in-law and I made it our Sunday morning outing. After putting the dirty clothes into the washing machines, one of us drove to Wolfie's delicatessen to get three Sunday morning specials (pancakes, eggs, and bacon). We had our communal breakfast on the clothes-folding table with the hum of the washers and dryers in the background. It was a great time to share the week's gossip.

Our expanded house design included a washer and dryer in the upstairs bathroom. Once the new laundry room was in place, the Sunday morning outings with the girls stopped. It was like the removal of the butcher-block table from the kitchen- something special was lost in the course of progress. It reminded me of an anthropological study about how a well-meaning group's installation of plumbing in a town in Africa upset their society. The women used to carry water on their heads from the wells and that was where young men went to court their prospective brides. All new rituals were needed to replace the "well courting" because spigot flirting didn't "hold water" to flirting at the well.

My household "To-do List" started in 1979 with "Purge any and all traces of Ex-wife" and "Rid house of Bachelor Days' collections." It contnued with "Clean, but with sensitivity (one person's bent hanger is another's boot rack)." By 1981, the house was ready to welcome children. We experienced the homeowner's reality; that maintaining a house would be a never-ending task in order for Castle Nanos to be completed. We had the additional challenge of living at sea level at the mercy of the storms and tides.

Enter reality. I didn't marry Michael Landon, my house was
a 1950-something Cape Cod with vinyl siding

All of this lush growth was made possible through the miracle of composting.

FIVE

Breast Pumps and Brief Cases

While making our home ready for a family, I was setting up my law practice with the goal of becoming a working mother. Young women reading this need to transport themselves to another time and another mindset. In 1981, women were still a novelty in law and the concept of a woman dividing herself between career and family was not fully defined. The first time I went into a courtroom at Nassau Supreme Court, I took a seat in the back behind a sea of middle-aged men and wondered what I was doing there. I didn't plan to change my gender and could not change my age but I began to wish for a few strands of distinguishing gray hair.

In college in the 70's, one of my best friends took a summer job pumping gas. You might ask from today's perspective why she would have done that. What could be more unpleasant than tending gas pumps in the summer heat? There was only one reason: because she *could* and nobody could stop her from doing any job that a man could do. Up until that time, women's occupations were a narrow list of acceptable vocations with teaching and nursing at the forefront.

My mother was a registered nurse and urged me to be a school-teacher. Life was so much simpler when there were fewer choices.

My college friend was proud of her gas station jump suit and newly acquired squeegee skills. Today, forty-seven percent of Juris Doctors are women and it started with breaking down stereotypes by pumping gas. Betty Friedan, in her 1963 groundbreaking book The Feminine Mystique, debunked the belief that women should find identity and meaning solely through husband and children. According to her, this belief led to widespread depression and feelings of emptiness. She introduced the idea that it was a woman's right to seek her own personal fulfillment in stark opposition to the prevailing norms.

Friedan was born the year after women received the right to vote and she stood on the strong shoulders of that first wave of suffragettes who fought against being second-class citizens. She took the battle one step further to improve lifestyle. We were the vanguards in the second wave sexual revolution. Fifty years after women won the right to vote, I was in law school. I learned how to pick a jury just one year after the Supreme Court ruled that women could no longer receive an automatic exemption from jury duty. There are always "firsts" for women. In Nassau County where I reside, we elected our first woman District Attorney and a woman County Executive. Our state has women Senators and Representatives.

I was one of the lucky ones who passed the Bar Exam first time around, but it was far from smooth sailing. Before I was officially admitted to practice law, I began to work with Margie, a lawyer who was also recently married. We wanted to build an immigration practice capitalizing on my ability to speak Spanish and her Chinese background. The eastern and western hemispheres would be represented.

The office that Margie and I found was inside a professional suite. We couldn't be fancy because we didn't have any client following; we were hanging up a shingle on a door without a foundation. I actually think that our office was just a passageway. I came to this conclusion from the following evidence: There was another person renting in the room behind us who had to walk through our office to get to his, the gas meters were in our closet, and there was a sink in our office. Despite all that, we made it very presentable. Nick put up shelves for a set of law books and we bought a desk and chair, voila.

I got myself into trouble right out of the gate. I was naïve and uninitiated in this new career arena. We had a reception in our new office. I made the mistake of sending an invitation with my name listed on the letterhead, even though I was only allowed to be a paralegal until my swearing-in ceremony. One of my law school fellow students resented my jump-start and reported me. I have heard enough lawyer jokes to know that many people don't think there is a moral benchmark for lawyers, but we all had to be approved by the Committee on Character and Fitness to be admitted to practice. I was called to go before the full Character and Fitness Committee to explain myself.

The day of my hearing before the Committee may have been one of the most frightening experiences of my life. The possibility existed that my four years of driving to class at night, studying on weekends, and scrimping to get by without a full time job could end in a decision by the Committee that I was not fit to practice. I had allegedly engaged in the unauthorized practice of law. One lawyer I know who had a challenge made to her admission hired an attorney to represent her at a cost of several thousand dollars.

Perfectly in character, I asked a friend who had given up his worldly possessions for spiritual practices to pray and meditate for me. As strong as my spiritual support was, I shudder to think that I faced this challenge without legal representation. I sat in the waiting room with weak legs and racing heartbeats. You may not believe in the power of prayer, but I suddenly felt a wave of calmness flow through me, and by the time my name was called, I walked into the room feeling inexplicably confident.

I was before a tribunal, not of my peers.

"Can you please explain to us why your name appeared on the letterhead of a law office when you are not yet admitted to practice?"

"Yes, Sir. The attorney I work for was having a reception for the new office and I told her I would invite people I knew. I asked a friend to make up fifty pieces of letterhead with my name on it to send to family and friends."

"Wouldn't that lead people to believe you are a lawyer?"

"Everyone I sent to knew I hadn't been admitted. I didn't send it to any strangers."

"You sent that letter before you knew whether you had even passed the Bar Exam. Were you so sure you had passed?"

"It would have been against the odds if I hadn't. I was in the top half of my class and the passing rate for St. John's Law was 85-90%." Several members on the Committee exchanged glances of suppressed amusement. They didn't know what to make of this young female aspiring attorney with so much confidence, and I'm sure it would not have made it any clearer if I had told them that I had a yogi praying for me.

They sent me out of the room so that they could deliberate over my fate. I began to think about alternative career choices; the thought of starting over made me dizzy and weak. After what felt like an interminable time, I was called back having no idea what the outcome would be. The Chairperson addressed me, "We have decided that, after weighing all of the factors, you can go ahead and be admitted to practice." I thanked them all in a daze, walked out, and cried tears of relief. There is a Japanese saying that only artists and lawyers can change white to black. I could go ahead and buy my paintbrush. Lawyer jokes aside, I hold it to be a noble profession and can't imagine how different my life would have been had I been barred from practicing.

Once I was officially admitted to practice, I needed letterhead and a business card. I had decisions to make about how I wanted to be known professionally. The new feminism gave me the option of using my maiden name, my married name, or a combination of both, maybe hyphenated. I decided on my maiden and married, without a hyphen. Over the years, my maiden name has become reduced to a middle initial but, at least, it maintains some presence. Prior to the women's movement, women's maiden names disappeared entirely upon marriage.

In the Hispanic culture, which I had studied up close and personal, when women married they became "of" their spouse ("de"), denoting possession. If the spouse pre-deceased, the woman's name changed to "Viuda de," which translates to "Widow of." Even in death, the husband continued his claim to his wife. In American culture, women were often known by their husband's name. I have a photograph from 1932 of a family reunion in Tennessee of my mother's clan. My mother appears, at age ten, with her three siblings and her parents. Her mother is identified as, "Mrs. Scott Braden Weatherspoon." Her name, Annie Belle, was lost to posterity. The sexual revolution made a valid point in questioning these patently male traditions.

As it turned out, immigration law attracted many women and Margie and I were not unique as females in the field. It wasn't uncommon to find myself as the defense attorney facing a female prosecutor in proceedings presided over by a female judge. On more than one occasion, I thought I would rather be hanging out with these women than arguing a case, but then we would power through our professional roles. We were all getting used to this new equilibrium.

What was unique about Yang and Nanos was not that we were female partners but that one of us was always pregnant! Besides our respective strengths for our immigration practice, our partnership was also formed with family planning in mind. We each wanted to have at least two children while continuing to practice and we didn't think any employer would be willing to hire an associate who immediately needed two maternity leaves. The introduction of women in professions was creating a host of new issues in the workplace.

Women are more often than not the ones to go "off-ramp" in their careers when they take time out for childcare. Corporate America offers on-ramp/off-ramp options for employees in order to keep talent in the marketplace. Margie and I had fashioned our own flex-time jobs ahead of this movement. We shared one desk; she worked Tuesdays and Thursdays and I worked Mondays, Wednesdays, and Fridays.

My son, Ian, was my first born. While I was nursing, I stored small packets of breast milk in the home freezer to be fed to him while I was at the office. My life had progressed from the frozen LSD of my college years to breast milk in my freezer. It hardly seems possible when I think back that I brought a pump to work so that, on my lunch break, I could relieve the pressure of the milk engorging my breasts, but that was my reality. My breast pump was hand operated like I was playing a slide trombone, not like an electric pump that lactating moms use today.

One friend, who was also dedicated to breast feeding her baby while maintaining her career, recalled pumping her breasts at 5:00 a.m. in order to get to work on time. On her first day back to work, she struggled to express two ounces of milk, but in her early morning rush, she knocked it onto the floor. She sat down and began to cry. While the expression about not crying over spilt milk most assuredly was not anticipating that situation, it fit nevertheless.

Needing a private space to breast pump at work was one of the factors that motivated me to go into practice with another woman of child-bearing age. In those times, a woman who wanted to breastfeed would have been banished to a dusty storage room or unsanitary bathroom stall. In 2010, the federal Affordable Care Act specifically addressed breastfeeding by requiring employers to provide reasonable break time and a private space for pumping, nearly forty years after I balanced my breast pump and brief case.

When Nick and I thought the time was right to have a second child, I became very strategic about when our new addition should be born. My life was now more complicated with one child and a growing law practice. I calculated that if our second child were born at the beginning of the summer, Nick, who worked on an academic calendar, would be home from work to help with childcare. "Doing what comes naturally" with the benefit of calendars and sensitivity to ovulation cramps was not sufficiently reliable for my working mother schedule.

I started taking my temperature to pinpoint the exact time when I could conceive. I had charts that I kept daily. This type of family planning requires sex on demand, which may not sound like such a terrible thing, but it was unromantic. It was not as stressful as what some couples undergo with artificial or in vitro insemination, but it was still clinical because, when my temperature rose, even if we were engaged in a Cold War, we had to have a détente.

Our daughter, Rhea, was born on the first day of Nick's summer vacation. We couldn't have timed it more closely than that. What we didn't time perfectly was getting to the hospital. We chose to have midwives deliver our children. It was already the eighties but we were still in hippie mode. I wanted the security of being in a hospital so we traveled from Nassau County to a university hospital in Brooklyn where midwives practiced in the hospital. The university hospital also had rooming-in, which allowed mothers to keep their babies with them instead of lining them up in an institutional nursery.

It was an hour's drive in normal traffic. The midwife told Nick to keep me at home as long as possible and he miscalculated. I was screaming for most of the ride to the hospital to pull over so I could have the baby. Rhea came very close to being born in the car on the shoulder of the Belt Parkway. One friend was told by her doctor not to leave for the hospital "until your knees buckle". She kept waiting for that sensation. It was all pretty awful and she wasn't sure if what she was experiencing reached the level of "knee-buckling." Suddenly she was into transition, her water broke, and like me, she arrived to a chorus of "Hold back, don't push" until they could prepare to receive the newborn. An intern delivered the baby before her obstetrician arrived.

Our newborn daughter had both parents home to cater to her for the first two months of her life but then it was time for us to return to our respective jobs. After I returned to work from having baby number two, my partnership with Margie ended. She had a very long commute, and as soon as we had both fulfilled our commitment to cover for each other's maternity leaves, she left to practice out of her home. Although our partnership ended, the legacy of hormones as a driving force in my law practice persisted for years to come.

Anyone who has experienced being a career mom knows that it requires a great deal of juggling. It was difficult to find any time for myself between the office and the children, but I was determined to try. I signed up for a meditation class in order to de-stress. On the first night of class, I tried to rush the breast-feeding. People do speed walking and speed reading, but I learned that speed breast-feeding wasn't recommended. I picked up Rhea to burp her and she threw up on me. I was late already, so I took a wash cloth, cleaned off my shirt and left for my class. With the aid of Indian music and incense, I set about clearing my mind and breathing deep, yogic breaths.

If you have ever practiced yoga, you know about diaphragmatic breathing. You enhance the inhalation by pushing out the diaphragm, thereby expanding the chest cavity. On each enhanced inhalation, I was acutely aware of the baby cheese stench on my shirt. I became paranoid and wondered whether I was the only one who could smell it because it was right under my nose. That question was answered when the instructor walked over to me and opened the window on the wall just above where I was seated. I was too embarrassed to ever go back.

There were other efforts to squeeze in time for myself including Weight Watchers meetings that were usually just weigh and run or nail appointments that often ended in smeared polish. No matter what I tried to do for myself, the effort of getting to the class, meeting, or appointment always seemed to create more stress than it was worth.

One activity I did with Ian and Rhea on my days off was to go to a Playgroup with five other moms and their children. Besides giving the babies a chance to have social interaction, the mothers socialized and shared information from diaper rash to teething problems. When I was growing up in the fifties, my mother didn't join a playgroup. My neighborhood was a new development built for World War II veterans who were starting their Baby Booming families and needed housing. All of the adults were roughly in the same age range with children in the same stages. The mothers naturally "coffee klatched" with their babies and the older children played together in packs. Our entire neighborhood was a playgroup.

Our Play Group alternated houses, putting out a luncheon for the Moms and appropriate kiddie foods for the tykes. The boys and girls enjoyed a change of scenery and the chance to interact with each other and play with different toys. We did art projects with them on holidays and celebrated birthdays. From one day to the next, I switched between cutting paper for arts and crafts projects with safety scissors to cutting legal arguments with carefully crafted language on paper.

On my workdays, I had a babysitter named Connie who lived across the canal from us. At first, she watched Ian at her house, a very warm and loving atmosphere. Connie, who was born and raised in Portugal, had an old country approach to things. I was humbled by someone who did anything from scratch: a skirt without a pattern, a cake without a mix; it was second nature to her.

With a toddler and an infant, getting both out of the house in the morning so that I could get to work became more difficult. This was compounded by the fact that Rhea, as an infant, finger-painted with her own poop. The first time I came to get her out of her crib and found the wall decorated artistically with excrement, I went into a panic.

It wasn't the mess that appalled me. If you are squeamish before having children, you quickly learn to overcome that sensitivity. After the first six months of childcare, you become adept at cleaning up the three P's: poop, pee, and puke. You learn to suck boogers out of the baby's nose with a suction device. You might even forget that these things once might have disgusted you.

What had me in a tizzy was that this was a setback for getting to work on time. I had to hose Rhea down in the shower, wash the walls and crib, and then get dressed in my suit. After that morning, I listened very carefully for the sounds of Rhea's first stirrings so that I could get up and change her diaper before she began to express herself. The artist in her was irrepressible. She learned to be very quiet, so that like a stealth bomber, she could wake up and paint without being picked up by mom's radar. We asked our babysitter Connie to watch the two children in our house instead of hers. I would leave the stealth bomber to her.

Connie's role grew from babysitter to housekeeper. She took on more and more responsibility over the years until it reached the point that she was food shopping, doing laundry, cooking, cleaning, and sewing. I sometimes came home to find she had re-arranged our furniture more to her liking. Her meals were a gourmet fare on a nightly basis. She was the only person I knew who made homemade French fries. Melanie's children didn't know that French fries came from potatoes until they visited my house. If what Connie prepared for us was too exotic for the children, she heated up fish sticks and chicken nuggets from the freezer for them and Nick and I dined on shrimp scampi or stuffed meatloaf.

From 1981 to 1985, my "To-do List" read, "Hang up Shingle: Lawyer for Hire," "Don't forget to put breast pump in brief case," and "Hire babysitter-it wouldn't hurt if she happens to cook, clean and sew." I look back now at those times as golden years when my life was a beautiful balance of career and family. I didn't know it was a fragile bubble.

What was unique about Yang and Nanos was not that we were female partners but that one of us was always pregnant!

SIX

From the Back Seat of the Gladiator

There are many books written on child rearing, but there is nothing to prepare someone like myself, who had absolutely no contact with children, for the actual experience. When I was a teenager, one couple hired me to babysit their infant. This was before Pampers disposables; we were still using cloth diapers with safety pins. When the baby wet himself, I couldn't figure out how to put on his diaper so I just covered him up with a blanket and didn't tell the parents when they got home that he was in his crib without a diaper. I can imagine that their discovery may not have been very pleasant. In any event, I was never called back to baby-sit there.

Our culture fosters female isolation. In other societies, especially in former times, women performed chores together, cared for each other's children, and even shared husbands. Families were extended and women could turn to their mothers, mothers-in-law, and sisters for advice and support. In the book, The Red Tent, which took place in the time of the Book of Genesis, there was a tent where women went when they menstruated, gave birth, or nursed. Men had several wives to lay with while their other partners were in isolation. It all made sense in the cultural context and the beauty of the sisterhood is what stands out.

To compensate for the lack of extended family support in our era, there are Lamaze classes to instruct on natural childbirth. We have La Leche League to teach about one of the most natural human functions, breast-feeding. Then come the Mommy and Me groups like my playgroup. I availed myself of all of these plus reference books and still managed to traumatize my children. Poor Ian, the first-born, felt the brunt of it.

Once I put Ian's car seat into the back of the car and fastened the buckle around his waist. I drove along and glanced occasionally into the rear view mirror to check on him. After taking a wide turn, I looked into the mirror and Ian wasn't there. I quickly pulled over to the side of the road and dashed out of the car to open the back door. While I had strapped the belt around Ian's waist, I hadn't buckled the chair onto the car seat. Ian was upside down in the back of the car, still strapped into his seat. I lifted him upright and he squealed with delight as I turned him right side up. "Wasn't that fun?" I asked him. I was relieved that he wasn't able to speak and tell Daddy what had happened, but the next time I goofed, I was not so lucky.

When I bought a new car with automatic door locks, I managed to lock Ian inside the car. How was I supposed to know that when you locked the passenger side, the driver side locked also? (I suppose the Owner's Manual might have been a starting point). Fortunately, I had turned on the air conditioning first to cool it down. I was visiting my mother on my old block. Ian was strapped into his car seat (this time, correctly) and he was amused by all of the neighbors gathered around the outside of the car, one of whom successfully unlocked the door with a hangar. When we got home, Ian, who was about two years old at the time, managed to string together enough of a sentence to alert Nick that there had been a problem: "Mommy-car door-uh-oh." Nick wanted me to fill in the details about the "uh-oh."

My lapses were mild in comparison to some I have heard about. One friend locked her daughter in the car ten times and was in the routine of carrying a hangar in her diaper bag. Another reported locking each of her two children in the car on separate occasions. I wish I had been privy to this information when Nick was berating my ineptitude.

Nick accused me of overcompensating for being a working mother and coddling the children when I was home. I never thought it was possible to give too much attention. His mother of six children once told me that it was all right to let a baby cry in his or her crib because "the baby was just exercising its lungs." That was horrifying to me. Even the pediatrician champion of infant tough love, Dr. Ferber, modified his stance on letting the baby cry. Researchers are making an argument that coddling enhances the development of a child's sense of security. Dr. Ferber conceded that there may be circumstances in which picking up a crying baby might be the right thing to do.

While I wasn't the most experienced mom (more likely the least experienced), I was still Ian's mommy and he loved the days when I was home from work to spend time with him. He watched carefully as I got ready in the morning and said, "Don't put on your stockings, Mommy." He had made the connection that if I put on stockings in the morning it meant I was going to my office; socks meant I was staying home. I became concerned that he was obsessing over stockings when he asked me sweetly one day if he could put on a pair. This was a tough call. I didn't want to make an issue about it and have him develop a sordid fetish or lead to cross-dressing.

"Boys don't wear stockings," I told him trying to be very matter-of-fact.

He caught me off guard when he answered, "I'm going to sneak into your room when you're not looking and put them on." I thought for sure I had blown it, but to my knowledge, he never followed through on that.

The hardest part of mothering two children for me was dealing with their jealousy over my attention. I wasn't good at managing the two of them together; I did much better with each one individually. Once, Ian pushed Rhea down and I got so mad at him that I chased him up the stairs and swatted him with his windbreaker that I happened to have in my hand. When I shared this story, I found a common denominator in three stories of mothers who acted out of character. As in the case of Ian pushing Rhea, two other mothers confessed to lashing out at their older children when they threatened the younger one. One case in point is made more extreme by the fact that the mother in question is a nurse who taught childcare classes. She flew into a rage when her son bit the new baby, taking off after him and biting him, while asking, "How do you like it?" It seems that the instinct to protect our newborn young is so powerful that it can evoke an irrational reaction even from a trained professional.

As parents, we want to protect our young from the greatest harms to the smallest disappointments. I can remember the first time Ian burst into tears from disappointment. He was fourteen months old and we decided to take down the Christmas tree while he was napping. When we brought him back downstairs after his nap, that miracle of tinsel and ornaments had disappeared, and he was inconsolable because he didn't understand that the Christmas tree was not going to be a permanent fixture in our home. We realized the impossibility of shielding our children from life's hard knocks, from the biggest to the smallest. Life wasn't always going to be a holiday.

Parents are in such a position of power when it comes to molding and shaping our offspring. Nick and I made pronouncements before our children were born about how we would raise them. It is popular to say to pregnant women that it doesn't matter whether you have a girl or a boy as long as the baby is healthy. Of course that is true, but I don't think there is a pregnant woman alive who doesn't secretly hope for one or the other. For me, I didn't know if I would relate to a boy, so I thought I would want to have a girl more. Once Ian was born, I adored him more than anything else in the world and found that it was easy to love a baby boy. When Rhea was born, I thought I would burst from the joy of having a little girl and always felt lucky to have a child of each sex, because as it turned out, raising them provided very different experiences.

I set out to treat my children in a non-sexist way. I favored primary colors or pastel yellow or green over the traditional pinks or blues. Nick and I agreed that we wouldn't give our children guns to play with since we both thought this was an inappropriate toy. I began to observe that Ian fashioned guns out of every toy he had. A plastic totem pole ended up being aimed at imaginary targets and Legos were assembled to resemble rifles. We eventually gave in and bought him toy guns.

Rhea, on the other hand, enjoyed flipping through my catalogs. One day she said, "Mommy, I like the white ones." White ones? I went to see what she was looking at and, sure enough, she had a page filled with diamond jewelry opened up in front of her. She was destined to be a high maintenance woman. I didn't even wear a diamond engagement ring, so I really wondered if it was genetically programmed that diamonds are a girl's best friend. I had to modify my thinking on sexual programming, as it seemed unavoidable. It was either genetic or subtly transmitted in everything we did or said, and all that they absorbed from their surroundings.

When potty training was the main topic of conversation, we had a potty-chair front and center in our living room. We encouraged Ian and Rhea to sit on the chair while they were playing at the coffee table so they didn't miss any fun. Our idea was that once they got the hang of it, we could move the activity into the bathroom. One of our neighbors complained when he had guests over in his backyard because we had a potty-chair out in the kids' sandbox. I can empathize with him. He was entertaining on his waterfront deck and he had to listen to, "Wow, look at that poop!"

In contrast to my inexperience, Nick was very comfortable with childcare duties. He came from an Irish Catholic family. He and his next-in-line brother were eleven months apart in age. That meant that when his mother registered them for school she had to say she had two children born in the same year who were not twins. Seven years later, Tommy was born, and over time, earned the nick-name General Nuisance. Then came Patricia, Ron, and the last child, Renae, who was born when Nick was a freshman in college. She was nick-named Rhythm, which was not at all fair since her parents' birth control methods were not her fault.

Nick had the benefit of experience in his back pocket. When Ian stuck a vitamin up his nose, I screamed, "Oh, my God, call 911!" Nick walked into the kitchen, got the pepper shaker and put pepper in Ian's nose whereby he sneezed out the vitamin. I would never have thought of that. None of the books I read talked about babies stuffing things up their noses, but it is apparently not a unique occurrence. One friend fished a raisin out of her son's nostril with a car key, definitely not recommended. My morning radio program had listeners call in revealing items they had extracted from children's noses. It turned out to be quite an extensive list: Tic Tacs, crayons, beads, and beans, to name a few.

What made Nick's approach to parenting noteworthy was his ability to pursue his own interests while engaging the children in them, an ability honed through many years of dealing with General Nuisance and the other younger siblings. My mother was the one who said that teaching was a great career to mix with raising a family, though in our house, Nick was the teacher with the summer months off. For him, summers had always meant fishing and gardening, and he wasn't about to let children cramp his style. When he gardened, he simply ran a hose into the sandbox and let the children dig channels through it. They were so dirty by the time I came home from work that we had to shower them and wash their hair outdoors so as not to clog the bathtub drain.

As for the fishing, Nick purchased a small, used cabin cruiser. He loaded the children on board and took them out for the day with their toys and peanut butter and jelly. On any given summer day, Ian was in charge of peanut butter and jelly sandwiches. He made up a tray of them and cut them into quarters to snack on. Nick would mash them down after they were made, mixing the peanut butter with the jelly to make sure the children ate both, not just the sweet jelly. When one peanut butter company made their product with jelly swirled through it, Nick pointed out that he had been the first with that idea and probably lost thousands of dollars by not patenting it.

We agreed to limit the amount of time our children watched television. If they could be outside, they generally were, but when it was time to come indoors, there were Legos and costumes for creative play. I was a big fan of Sesame Street and often watched it with Ian and Rhea. Muppets were all right by me. I am eternally grateful that I was not a mother of the dancing purple dinosaur generation, but I did have to endure Dr. Who, a cult British science fiction program that captivated Nick and the children.

I didn't entirely get Dr. Who. I could identify the household products used to create the special effects, such as vacuum cleaner hoses. Talk about low budget: the space ship, the TARDIS (Time and Relative Dimension in Space), resembled a British telephone booth on the outside and miraculously expanded to a full size room upon entering. The actors playing Dr. Who were on a revolving door basis, so a phenomenon was created whereby Dr. Who had several lifetimes and was continually regenerating.

The sharing of Nick's enthusiasm for Dr. Who with Ian and Rhea had self-serving motivation. He could pretend that our king size bed was the space ship TARDIS and have the children bring all of their toys on board while he brought his newspaper to read-cover to cover. Had he simply sat at the kitchen table reading the paper, they would have nagged him mercilessly to pay attention to them, but on the TARDIS bed, everyone entertained himself or herself; it was a matter of survival. I'm jealous that Nick managed to fish, garden, and read the paper when he watched the children while I catered to them endlessly taking them to gymnastics, birthday parties, and library reading club.

The picture of our household would not be complete without adding a few animals. Rhea had a long history of acquiring pets, and as we all know, when your child gets a pet, you end up taking care of it even though you begin by thinking this is going to teach your child responsibility: your pet, your job. We had a menagerie of pets. I fed and cleaned their bowls, beds, tanks, and cages. The Belgium rabbit, Mr. Moustache, was one of the more exotic animals that Rhea had in her bedroom over the years. It dawned on me recently that when Rhea asked for a new pet, I could have said "no." I never did.

Our home would have been much neater without multiple cats. We had cat doors so that the cats could come and go as they pleased during the daytime hours. In our den, there were cat bowls lined up which were filled with food every morning and night. The wild opossum from our waterfront property began to treat our house as a local feeding station. One by one, they were caught in a Have-a-Heart trap and brought to the local pond to be released. They probably sat around a campfire, reminiscing about the good ole days on Farmers Avenue when meals were served twice daily with a selection of surf, turf, or fowl in glass bowls lined up for their pleasure.

When my favorite chubby female cat was killed by a car, my sister-in-law, Patricia, invited me to her house to see their new litter of kittens. There were two males left, sleeping together like a Yin and Yang. Rhea didn't want to separate them so I came home with both. Nick warned me that they disturbed the male/female balance among the cats and we now had too many males. The largest male cat exercised his dominance by spraying anything new that came into the house. It was perfectly acceptable behavior in the cat world. If he were a teenager, he might write with graffiti, "Norman was here." If he were a human adult, he might leave his business card. But he was a cat. Imagine if he had a business card. It would read, "Norman, Top Cat. Specializing in eradication of birds and small rodents. I can be reached at my office on the front porch, wicker rocking chair." Spraying worked fine for his purposes. A cat will act like a cat and there was a lesson in that to apply to child rearing.

At a birthday party for Ian, we served hamburgers and Jell-O. I left the dining room for a minute, and when I returned, there was a Jell-O food fight in progress. Later, I commented to Nick, "I can't believe the boys misbehaved like that." He asked me, "What did you expect, that they were going to talk politics?" Little boys will act like little boys. It makes no sense to complain about the rain being wet or a rock being hard. Jell-O food fights turned out to be innocuous by comparison to some of the later years' antics.

In our community, school-aged children were generally sent to summer camps. When our children began to ask why they didn't go to camp, Nick told them to say that they went to Camp Nick. "No camp," he said, "could compare to a day out on the boat eating squished peanut butter and jelly or a rainy afternoon of watching Dr. Who." Ian and Rhea also asked why we didn't take family vacations like their friends did. Some of them went on cruises with their parents or stayed at resorts. It was always my position that the term "family vacation" is an oxymoron. These vacations are overrated at best, and in my family's case, a disaster.

If the four of us went for a car ride, we didn't even clear the block before Ian started. "I'm car sick," he would say from the back seat.

"I'm hot," Rhea would add.

My response to both would be, "Open the window a crack," but Nick would object to opening the window in the summer, because it let out the air conditioning and in the winter, because it let out the heat. The chorus of complaints would continue until Nick turned up the radio to drown it out. It's no wonder I referred to the car as the "torture chamber."

I had a model for the automobile torture chamber from road trips when I was a child. Because my mother was born and raised in Tennessee, we went south every year to visit my grandmother. Remember that these journeys took place back in the days when having air conditioning in a car was a luxury item. We drove for three days in the sweltering heat, my brother Mark and I sharing the back seat. He entertained himself by tormenting me with annoying pinches until I whined, "Stop it, Maaaark!" It could have been an opportunity for my parents to encourage me to develop assertive and effective behavior to stop my brother; instead, they invariably yelled at me for whining and my brother got away with pinching.

My father, a news addict, listened to 24-hour news radio when we were in the car. By the tenth time of hearing the same story repeated, I was ready to jump out of the moving vehicle and myself become the next late breaking news: "This just in: Long Island girl jumps out of moving car. Witnesses at the scene report that she kept babbling, 'Coming up next, your local news.'" An excursion in the car with my own kids must have felt too reminiscent of the pain of my childhood road trips.

In view of the fact that we didn't enjoy road trips, it was puzzling that Nick bought an extra-long van with plush carpeting, curtains, captain's chairs, and a television in the back. I think he was suckered in by the name that appeared in large letters across the windshield which appealed to his combative side. The decal identified our van as "THE GLADIATOR." He was so proud of the van that I couldn't resist parking it down the block on April Fool's Day and acting as if someone had stolen it.

Rhea's friends asked to be picked up in The Gladiator because we could fit so many of them into the back. I tried to avoid being seen driving the van; I donned sunglasses and pulled a hat down low on my forehead to travel incognito, but who was I fooling? There was only one Gladiator in in our town.

When it came time to sell The Gladiator, I found out the true meaning of a white elephant, a costly item that no one wants. It was large enough to haul cargo, but the customized interior made it impractical for even the most basic trip to the dump. After ten years, Nick had to face the fact that there was no Coliseum in our town; he succumbed to family pressure and sold his cherished van. The sale of the Gladiator marked the end of an era for our family. When the children realized the absurdity of the van and began to complain about it, we realized that their innocent years of being malleable, fragile, dependent beings were over.

If you ask either of our children whether they enjoyed their childhood, I feel certain they will say an emphatic "yes." When looking through the volumes of photo albums we kept when they were growing up, you see they are filled with pictures of camping trips, trick-or-treating, birthday parties, and favorite pets. As you flip through the pictures, the backyard pool grows with Ian and Rhea in one-foot increments from a wading pool to a four-foot high oval occupying a quarter of our backyard. There was a spot of dried Jell-o on the ceiling for years.

There were costumes that I loved making, some worn with more gusto than others. When Ian was seven or eight years old, he landed the role of the chicken in a play alongside his sister who was the cow. Rhea had her outfit to a tee down to the cowbell around her neck. For Ian's costume, I bought a bright yellow sweat suit and yellow wool cap. In a dime store, I found yellow feather dusters, which I took apart and glued to the sweat suit. Right there in the same cleaning aisle there was a pair of yellow duster mitts to cover his hands. When he walked out on stage, his scarlet red face was the only part of him that wasn't Daffodil yellow. He was not a happy Thespian and enjoyed my creative Halloween costumes much more.

The ending of those childhood years came with another chapter closing when I was forty years old and suffering from on-going gynecological problems. My gynecologist suggested that I should have a laparoscopy to check out if all was well and he added, "While I'm already there, maybe I should close up shop."

"Close up shop?"

"I mean, you're not planning to have any more children, are you? So you might as well have a tubal ligation. You won't have to worry about birth control for the next ten years until menopause."

I have to admit that sounded attractive. Nick and I went for dinner at the diner across the street from the GYN's office and talked about it.

Nick was distraught. "I always wanted a third child."

"Honey, the reality is that we aren't having anymore. We gave away the changing table and crib many years ago."

"But the finality of it . . ."

"The truth is that I barely made it through my second pregnancy, suffering from gestational diabetes and anemia, and I was only thirty-three then. Imagine me and childbirth at forty."

"You're right . . . Tell the doctor you'll go ahead."

During the first decade of childcare from 1982 to 1992, I checked off from my "To-do List:" "Learn to change diapers and potty train two children," "Drive kids around in The Gladiator."

Nick told them to say that they went to Camp Nick.

When Ian was seven or eight years old, he landed the role of the chicken in a play alongside his sister who was the cow.

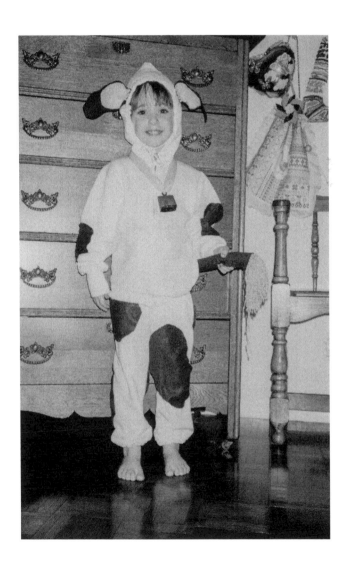

SEVEN

To Hug or Not to Hug: That Is the Question

Imagine a Loom of Life that weaves warp over weft to create a fabric of experience. From birth on, this imaginary loom absorbs the stimulus around us, processing it into threads for our personal weave. The choices we make as adults are often reactions to experiences in our childhood that we saw as strong threads or ones that came unraveled. For some, the resulting fabric is an exquisite silk brocade and for others a sturdy gabardine. I only hope that the fabric I weave for my life will not be a synthetic polyester blend.

Nick and I both chose to situate ourselves on Long Island in proximity to our extended families, a decision based on our own childhood experiences that, in turn, had a tremendous impact on our children. My parents lived nearby, only a fifteen-minute drive from our house. Ian and Rhea had their own set up of toys in my parents' basement and their special food treats in the refrigerator. I was at a street fair in our town recently and one of the booths was selling a garden ornament that was a directional pointing to "Grandma's house: Sleepovers, Hugs and Kisses, Cookies and Milk." That about summed it up. Nick's mother, on the other hand, raised six children over the span of thirty-five years and was very clear with me that she wasn't looking to extend her childcare years any further. I understood, but not without resentment.

Nick's brothers and sisters with their spouses all lived within a two-county radius, a fact that puzzled me at first. Since Nick considered himself to come from a bruised and battered family, I would have thought that they would want to get away from their unpleasant memories. Instead, they formed a bond of mutual support. We were incredibly close and raised our children together. Ian and Rhea had ten aunts and uncles to participate in their upbringing.

They were a colorful bunch. Nick's brother, Ron, was a jokester. When we drew names for gift giving at Christmas, he switched all of the names to his. When one brother said, "What should I get Ron?" his sister said, "What do you mean? I got Ron," and so the joke was exposed. When the older siblings had children before Ron did, he bought all of his nieces and nephews loud ray guns for Christmas that disturbed the peace of the holiday. Once he had his own children, he became Mr. Mom while his wife worked out of the home.

Ron made up a business card for himself: "Stay at home Dad and Fishing Enthusiast. Live, love, laugh, change diapers, and fish." The card had contact information for RONZO, Inc. and was pretty hilarious. Ron died an untimely death in his fifties from cancer that knocked the close knit family for a loop. At his wake, the minister asked for remembrances. My son, fast forwarding to adulthood by then, recounted how he used to go out fishing with his uncle who nicknamed him the Master Baiter. Really, Ian? At a wake? The minister cringed, and for just a brief instant, I looked at the coffin to see if there was room for me to jump in. But everyone at the wake loved Ron and had a good laugh at the memory.

Both of Nick's sisters spent time living in our house on Farmers Avenue, viewing their older brother as a surrogate father. His younger sister, Renae, graduated high school while at our house and his older sister, Patricia, spent about a year with us and eventually bought a house down the block. Tricia was at my side when I was in labor with Ian. Her first son spent summers at Camp Nick with cousins Ian and Rhea.

Tricia's favorite pass-times were cooking, eating, and drinking. She also loved to put tanning oil on her body and roast in the sun while reading a great novel. She is a large woman with ample bosom who stored things in her bra, which made Rhea and Ian uncomfortable when they were younger. They eventually became desensitized to it, to the point that Rhea hardly flinched, when in high school, she introduced her shy boyfriend to Aunt Tricia and Tricia pulled out a cigarette and lighter from between her breasts to have a smoke. The cigarette smoke caused the boyfriend to sneeze. In response, Aunt Tricia then retrieved a packet of tissues from deep inside her cleavage and offered it to him. The poor kid didn't know whether or not it was polite to take a treasure chest offering, but Rhea urged him to go ahead.

Once, Tricia recounted how someone backed into her in the parking lot.

"I couldn't believe this guy. I was shouting out my window, 'Watch where you're going, Asshole!' but his car hit me."

I posed a basic question, "Did you honk your horn?" The silence that followed led me to believe that this recommended defensive measure hadn't occurred to her.

In stark contrast to Nick's siblings who all stayed nearby, as an adult, my brother drew an imaginary line around New York and wouldn't come any closer than a long day's drive away. He has reminded me that "family" is not a word; it's a sentence. Since graduating from college, my brother has lived in four different states. The range of locales and homes has been expansive from a split-level in Colorado, a one-hundred-year-old farm house in southern Virginia, and most recently, a condo in California on Alameda Island. I pride myself on having visited him at almost every home he has lived in or owned. The one I missed in Kansas was very short-lived. He didn't realize that he was renting downwind from a meat packing plant and the smell was unbearable to the vegetarian members of his family.

There is one commonality in these homes; none was in proximity to my brother's birth family living on Long Island. A therapist asked me to try to explain this phenomenon of distance since I remembered my family as such a close, loving bunch. My best illustration was that my parents were so considerate they hired someone to feed the wild birds in their back yard when they went on vacation. I remember discussing this with them.

"You know, Mom and Dad, it isn't usual for people to hire someone to feed wild animals."

"But they have become dependent on us. If we just stop feeding them, they might go hungry . . ." (or learn to find a worm, I thought to myself).

The therapist understood that if my parents fostered dependence on the part of wild animals, one could only imagine their impact on their children. In order to be his own person, my brother distanced himself. He created a fascinating lifestyle as a professor, then Dean, Assistant Provost, and world traveler, taking risks along the way that are not in keeping with parental or sibling advice. When he returned to school to earn his doctorate, he moved his family in with friends and existed on almost no income for the time it took to complete his studies. My brother has been to China twice and was a visiting professor in countries that most of us couldn't locate on a map, like Azerbaijan. In my law practice, I handle asylum claims from clients who were persecuted in some of the countries he visited. "Mark, that former Soviet republic used to send people to the Gulag," I would remind him.

All of this risk-taking was probably much easier while living at a distance from his parents and sister. Nick's family didn't have to worry about anyone trying to offer them unsolicited guidance since they had all been on their own from the time they graduated high school, and some might say, quite a bit before that.

When I was growing up, my extended family included two couples who my parents knew since before they all had children. We socialized with their families so regularly that we referred to them as aunts and uncles. Uncle Lou was the fraternity brother whose little black book led my father to my mother's home on Ben Allen Road. My Aunt Shirley attended all of my family's functions well into her nineties. We children were all around the same age and were raised almost as cousins with Melanie and Janet becoming dear friends into adulthood. These bonds are ones that I cherished.

There is a fine line between togetherness and meddling that is often a matter of perspective. When I was a pre-teen, my aunt cornered me in her kitchen at a holiday gathering and performed a ceremonial first bra presentation. In attendance were my mother, another aunt, and my female cousin. My aunt had seen this little stretchy training bra in a store and thought it would be perfect to control my budding breasts . . . the ones I was hunching my shoulders to hide and hoping nobody had noticed. Aunt Lee had noticed.

My aunt undoubtedly remembered the moment as being one of female bonding, but I recall it as absolute mortification. A co-worker one-upped me on this type of extended family mortification. In her native Puerto Rico, the family made a big fuss when a girl began her period. Her father brought her flowers and her grandmother came for dinner to congratulate her on becoming a "senorita," while her five brothers snickered in the corner. It took many years of distance and perspective for her to be able to think back and laugh at the occasion.

Several women at a retreat group told me that they were surprised to receive a slap in the face when they informed their mothers they had their first period. This is apparently an Old World tradition in Jewish cultures, known as "minhag," which none of them could satisfactorily explain to me. As if discovering blood in your panties isn't traumatic enough, it was a bright idea to add the slap. Some of the suggested explanations for the slap were: to ward off evil, to remind that a woman's life is filled with pain, or to warn the young virgin to stay out of trouble now that she was in harm's way. The message was the exact opposite of the Puerto Rican view.

Menstruation was seen as taboo in the Jewish culture, not something to be celebrated. When I read The Year of Living Biblically by A.J. Jacobs, I learned, that in the Hebrew Bible, men were not supposed to have any physical contact with menstruating women. The author's wife compared it to theological "cooties." Some of my friends' mothers called the menstrual period "the curse." My mother, always so sweet and positive, told me that it meant I could have children one day.

I had a minimum amount of childhood trauma compared to many people I know including my husband and his family who frequently had the local police at their house to break up family disturbances. Everything about our two families is a study in contrast. Nick had a household of six siblings, with all of the squabbling rivalry that entails: get off the phone so I can make a call; it's my turn to pick what show we watch; I need to get into the shower . . . His parents were overwhelmed with bills and responsibilities and let the children work out their own conflicts. In my home, we didn't raise our voices to each other and spoke respectfully to one another.

The kids in the neighborhood described my clan as a TV family which, in those days, wasn't an insult. That was before All in the Family portrayed the first dysfunctional family in the 70's, followed by the Simpsons cartoon and Married with Children in the 80's-90's. My friends' frame of reference at the time was the Cleavers from Leave It to Beaver or the Andersons of Father Knows Best.

My mother called my father "Hon" and she was "Babe." Occasionally if my mother was annoyed with my father she called him "Jack" and if she wanted to *really* emphasize her displeasure, first and last name were used. He was lucky he didn't have a middle name because that would have given a weapon for further escalation. However, I never heard him call her anything but "Babe."

The use of pet names was second nature to me and I carried on the habit, calling Nick "Honey." Ian was confused about Nick's real name since I called him "Honey" but talked about him as "Dad," so Ian referred to him as "Honey-Dad" to cover all bases. Nick's pet-name for me was "Lovebug." He came up with that unique handle for me on his own and it is interesting to note that it combines the sentiment of affection with the concept of a pest. I was also referred to as "your mother" to the children, especially when I was being the bad guy as in "*Your mother* thinks it's time for us to get out of the pool." "*Your mother* thinks we've had enough ice cream." We were not above calling each other "Bitch" and "Asshole" under our breaths, but the most hurtful name he ever called me was Goody Two Shoes. Ouch!

Until fairly recently, I idealized my childhood because, on the surface, all seemed harmonious. Digging a bit deeper, I have to question the lack of outward displays of affection, especially as we grew older. When I was small, my mother held me and it felt warm and comforting. I have memories of my mother rubbing my feet when we watched television. One of my friends in elementary school had a hot mom; the kind the male teachers would have called a MILF, if the term had been invented at the time (Mother I'd Love to Friend . . . anticipating Facebook). I was glad my mother didn't look like that because the hot mom seemed unapproachable.

As my brother and I hit puberty, there was less holding and never kissing. My brother came home from college with a novel idea that he had picked up from observing his friends at school interacting with their families; we should hug one another. He demonstrated how it was done. The fact that we loved each other was understood and apparently, it was felt there was no need to physically demonstrate it or say it. My father tried to break the physical affection barrier with his grandchildren. Ian remembers Grandpa reaching over to pat his knee several times, and with each pat, my father drew his hand back so quickly it appeared he was avoiding an electric shock.

Nick's family not only hugs one another but also kisses, sometimes lip-to-lip, and they say they love each other. I am not the only one who was uninitiated into the world of hugs. We were at a wedding reception and Nick had drunk an open bar's worth of alcohol. When it came time to leave, he was hugging everyone to say goodbye. A guest at our table said that he was looking for an emergency exit so that he could leave without getting the full Nelson body hug from Nick.

I have always known that my mother's love was unconditional for me but my father was emotionally unavailable. When we did something he considered wrong, my Dad gave my brother and me disapproving looks, which we called the "double whammy." Nick's father disciplined him with a belt. The harsh look is preferable to a beating but emotional damage shouldn't be underestimated. My father was a nineteen-fifties kind of dad who provided for us but didn't play or get very involved in our day-to day lives.

The dynamics of our nuclear family can program us for the rest of our lives or until psychoanalysis. In my case, overcoming distance in relationships with males was a definite theme for therapy. I don't hold this against my father. He was a model of integrity who deserved our respect and we never doubted that. He was awarded the "Man of the Year" plaque by a coalition of community agencies in our town for his tireless volunteer activities and we were very proud of him. I believe that the baggage I carried as a result of our relationship was no more or less than most daughters have with their fathers.

I'm not sure that I really know what the challenges of my mother's life have been. I'm sure that leaving her family and coming to live in an extremely different cultural and ethnic environment had to be painful and the source of conflict but, for my parents' generation, it was important to present a front of strength and to not expose their frailties. I tried once to broach the subject of one summer that my mother, brother, and I spent in Tennessee at my grandmother's house while my father stayed in New York. When we came home, my father gave my mother a pearl ring.

As an adult looking back, I wondered what the dynamics of their relationship were. It was odd that we spent so long away, and my father, who wasn't the sentimental type, gave a gift of jewelry. The only thing I could be sure of was that, if there was a problem, my mother would never tell me. I wish I could have shared more of my parents' emotional lives. When my mom died, I spent many days clearing out her apartment. I found a note in my father's handwriting telling my mother how much she meant to him and apologizing for any hurt he had ever caused her. I felt embarrassed for my unintentional intrusion on their privacy. I threw the note out. Our parents, like us, are fragile individuals who did not have all of the answers. They struggled with their own issues just as we struggle with ours. In that knowledge, we should be able to find forgiveness for them. I hope for that kind of compassion from my children.

There is one challenge that I can be certain my mother faced, running a household on a shoestring budget. That was in the early years before she went out to work, when we depended on my father's new teacher salary to support our family of four. "Money didn't grow on trees," as my father was quick to remind us, but it sometimes came out of a dog's butt. When our pet Missy ate a ten-dollar bill, my father waited for her to poop and picked the pieces of currency from it. He soaked them in antiseptic and attempted to restore the bill. We were relieved when, like Humpty Dumpty, he couldn't put Alexander Hamilton back together again. Every ten-dollar bill would have been suspect and nobody would have offered to go on an errand to the store.

In the fifties, my mother stayed at home and I walked to our house from school at lunchtime. Nick's mother was never employed outside the house and raised six children with a budget of next to nothing. The siblings complained about their brown bag school lunches that consisted of one slice of luncheon meat on two slices of white bread and a piece of fruit; they were always hungry. I think it was remarkable that she managed to give them as much as she did.

My mother also did an admirable job of making something from nothing. One Chanukah, my parents gave me a gift of a doll on the first of the eight nights, and each night thereafter, a homemade outfit for the doll. That was my favorite Chanukah even though I am sure there were others later in our family life that were more bountiful. Mom was a leader of the Girl Scout troop and the Boy Scout pack. I took guitar lessons at the cultural arts program, went to arts and crafts at the Youth Council summer recreation program, and rode horseback with the Girl Scouts. One of my favorite memories is riding the trails on a horse and spotting a red winged blackbird flying across the path. Mom found whatever she could offer us that didn't cost much. I learned from raising my millennial generation children, that their material expectations would be very different.

These structured community activities notwithstanding, we still had a great deal of unscheduled time. Parents didn't run around taking their children places like they do today. Also, it was also a more innocent time when we could roam the streets and play at the stream at the dead end, unsupervised. We played neighborhood-wide games of hide-n-seek and ring-a-leevio across unfenced yards. There was one neighborhood drunk who used to come out of his house in his underwear to yell a slurred, "Hey, you kids, get off my property," but that just added to the fun and excitement. We usually saw our parents only when called in to have lunch or dinner.

At night, my friend Joanne and I put on talent shows under the street light. By day, I remember sitting with her on the curb and saying, "What do you want to do?" to which the reply was always, "I don't know, what do you want to do?" If I were asked to choose the color of the threads for a childhood weave, they would be muted tones. Maybe that is why I see myself as a "taupe" person. It was a gentle, quiet youth without extremes of joy or sorrow.

By the sixties, my mother began to work one day per week. She had a career as a registered nurse and didn't want to lose it. After being out of the work force for over ten years, she took a refresher course in nursing and got back into a hospital shift. I can still remember my disappointment when I turned the corner of my block and saw that the car was gone. My heart always sank that I couldn't share the day's events with her. I warmed up and served a pre-cooked meal to my brother and father; the responsibility helped me to mature. I'm sure the extra money she earned came in handy.

Everyone in our neighborhood was in a marginal income bracket so I didn't know anything different. In that sense, ignorance was bliss. My house was in a development built by the Levitt contractors for the returning WW II vets who were starting the families they had put on hold during those war years. There were two styles of houses in the development: the Cape Cod with an unfinished second floor for $12,000 or the fully finished split-level for $15,000. My parents liked the split level but the extra $3,000 was prohibitive so I grew up in the Cape Cod in Farmingdale.

My cousins' family used to go to the Bahamas on vacation. My aunt came home with a tan in the middle of the winter, wearing shell jewelry, and bearing gifts of straw bags. I had no idea what that was all about. Our main get-away from Farmingdale until my teen years was the annual summer trip to Tennessee. My parents' idea of a vacation was taking a different route each time and making it palatable by stopping at the Natural Bridge along the way. My father, always the science teacher, also liked to arrange a factory tour to see how things were made.

We didn't go to Disney World; my parents weren't amusement park people. I may have developed a Disney obsession that had to be satisfied on my own time and dime. In my wildest imaginings,

I couldn't picture either one of my parents on a roller coaster. My father also went to college during several summers to update his science knowledge and he took the family along. We spent one summer in a cottage in Amish country where I played softball in a cow pasture. The Amish boys made fun of me when I came up to bat, but in one of my proudest moments, I had a base hit.

My favorite memory from the annual Tennessee trips was the excursion we took deep into the mountains to visit my mom's hillbilly cousin, Molly. Her husband and foster son, Dell Wayne, had built the house themselves. All of the floors were uneven and the walls were papered with newspaper and magazines. There was an outhouse. We swam in a waterhole that had a homemade diving board; we worked up an appetite. Molly served us dinner of an unidentified meat, most likely freshly killed with the shot gun on the porch (hopefully not road kill). My mother warned us not to ask but possum, squirrel, rabbit, and raccoon are all good guesses since they were within gunshot while the nearest supermarket offering beef was a half-day's drive away. An unforgettable, fresh-picked blackberry cobbler followed this mystery meat.

On one journey to the south, my mother decided to keep an account of every penny we spent so we wouldn't frivolously burn through our money. It was all going very well until we had a car accident on the way home and were towed to a cowpoke town off the highway. My parents had a decision to make:

"I say we buy bus tickets for the rest of the trip and purchase a car when we get home," my father said.

"Then we have the extra cost of the bus tickets and still need to buy a car. I think we should just look at cars here and buy one."

"That means the dealer has to trust us to give him a good check and we have to trust the dealer to sell us a decent car." This was before widespread use of credit cards. They decided to buy a car on the spot. Being in a farm town, they found that most of the cars smelled as if they had been used to transport livestock. They finally found one that ran well and didn't smell like a barn. My mother's vacation accounting ledger read: five cents for gum, fifty cents for soda, nine hundred dollars for car. Our Loom of Life operated on an austerity budget.

If I were to write a "To-do List" to improve on the early years of my life, it would read something like this: "hug each other," "wear shell jewelry and carry straw bags," "never reconstitute digested currency," "go to amusement parks," and "revel in extended family, for better or for worse."

I posed the question to a group of women as to what type of fabric would best represent each of their lives. One answered that corduroy with its ridges would reflect the ups and downs she has experienced. Another imagined a homespun cotton or linen would remind her of her earthy roots in the Philippines. A third member saw her fabric with dangling items such as shells, feathers, and beads like the collection of experiences of her life.

My group wanted me to choose a fabric. When I said that I didn't want to be an artificial polyester blend, they insisted that I choose what I wanted to be, not what I didn't want. Since I am revealing much of myself, I chose a sheer chiffon. I would hope my children would choose a comfortable fabric for their childhood weave, one in which they could envelope themselves, made from resilient thread in bright shades of Technicolor, like a Disney cartoon.

I see myself as a "taupe" person. It was a gentle, quiet
youth without extremes of joy or sorrow.

EIGHT

Desperately Seeking Disney

I t was Disney World or Bust. It was a rite of passage, which I had missed, and I was determined that my children would not. In 1992, when Ian and Rhea were ten and seven years of age, it seemed to be the perfect time to plan the Disney Odyssey.

Nick couldn't join us because he had a commitment to act in an amateur production of "Man of La Mancha" that opened during our four-day trip. It was not as if he were playing Don Quixote. He was one of the rapists who assaulted Dulcinea. I'm sure a stand-in could have performed equally as well, if he had actually wanted to join us. It was never *his* idea to go to Disney. Nick was skeptical about my ability to manage the trip on my own with the two children, but I reassured him. I reminded him (and myself) that I had traveled solo to the Galapagos Islands.

In a way, it was a relief that it wouldn't be a two-parent trip with a disagreement at every turn as to how, what, when, and where. Nick and I were always convinced of our own points of view. I bought a sign for Nick to hang next to his desk that posed the question in the

Daoist tradition, "If a man yells in a forest and there is no woman there to hear him, would he still be wrong?" I would answer, "Yes."

I knew that Ian and Rhea would complain about being tired, then hungry, and later hot, as it was inevitable when spending the day at an amusement park with children. Nick would have no patience for it and he would tell them to stop whining whereas I would want to find a way to ease the discomfort. I viewed myself as their spokesperson and advocate, defending against his no-nonsense ways, which were too reminiscent of his strict upbringing. It seemed that the children did fine when they were with either one of us; the problems arose when they could play us against each other. The dynamic was much simpler with one parent in charge. I am probably one of the few married women who took her children to Disney World by herself.

An amusement park venue, no matter how elaborate, was not Nick's idea of a good time. Once I made the mistake of planning an outing to a Renaissance Fair on Father's Day thinking it would be an entertaining family day. Watching jousting competitions in the broiling sun made for a miserable time for all. The fact that it was Father's Day and Nick would have been happier out on his boat compounded his annoyance. He wanted to impale me with one of those lances by the end of the afternoon. Same as my father, Nick was not an amusement park type person.

It astounded me at times, how I had managed to marry my father. Physically they are opposite ends of the spectrum, my Dad had a Mediterranean look and Nick had a fair, Irish complexion. I believed that, with Nick, I had broken the mold of attraction for dark, emotionally unavailable men. As it turns out, Jack and Nick were more alike than I cared to admit. Both were science teachers who loved gardening and relating to the environment. Neither cared for social amenities. Both were highly critical of their spouses and children.

Nick, like my father, is a news-aholic, reading two newspapers cover-to-cover on a daily basis. The day he called me from the car with the news station in the background on the car radio was when I realized I had not escaped Freud's psychoanalytic model that individuals choose partners who resemble their opposite sex parents.

To avoid the crowds on the Disney trip, I signed Ian and Rhea out of school. Off-season, we would be able to visit all of the attractions in three days. Our flight to Florida was delayed several hours until almost midnight. I had two sleeping children to get on board when they finally announced our departure. Once we arrived, I rented a car and set out to find our hotel on unfamiliar roads, in the dark. Before leaving New York, there had been several well-publicized incidents of sniper shootings on the highways of Florida. I had trouble finding the hotel and both children were over-tired, scared, and crying in the back seat. We were not starting out on a very magical note getting to the Magic Kingdom. We made it to our destination by about three a.m.

The former evening's tribulations were quickly forgotten the next morning when we awoke to a gorgeous tropical day and breakfast poolside. The hotel we stayed in was top notch with a kiddie slide in the pool that went through a waterfall. We were excited to set out on our adventure of exploring Disney World. It was more beautiful and enjoyable than I could have ever imagined.

Before we left the hotel each morning, I made sure I had all of my keys and my amusement park passes. I didn't forget the sunscreen. We had a perfect stay. When it was time to leave, I consulted my handy wallet-sized itinerary and left with time to spare to return my leased car and catch our flight. I checked our bags with the red cap by the curb and went inside the terminal to get our boarding passes.

Since I have labeled this trip as the Disney Odyssey, one would expect there to be obstacles to overcome. Odysseus had to battle the Cyclops and resist the temptation of the Sirens' singing that could lure him to his death. There can be no Odyssey without adversity. When we stepped up to the counter in the airport to get our boarding passes for our return flight, the clerk informed me our plane had just left, and to make matters worse, our bags had made it to the airplane even if we had not. I forgot that there had been a flight time change subsequent to purchasing my tickets and I never noted it on the handy wallet itinerary.

I called home. "Nick, the plane to New York just left and we weren't on it."

"WHAT! You missed your flight?"

"Calm down; it will be all right. The airlines is giving us a voucher to stay for free in a hotel next to the airport so we can catch a flight out tomorrow morning."

"I knew you . . ."

"Nick, stop. Everything else went really well. This was the only little glitch in our stay."

"Some *little* glitch."

"There is something else. Our luggage is on the plane that took off and will be arriving without us at the airport in a few hours. I need for you to either go and pick it up or call the airport for them to hold it for us."

"This is so typical. You come up with a great plan and I'm left holding the bag!"

"Bags, actually. There are three of them."

"I'm glad you can have a sense of humor. Anything else?"

"Yes, Hon, could you please call the school and tell them Ian and Rhea will be out one more day?" No response. "I love you."

Silence.

"Do you love me, Nick?"

"Of course, but you don't make it easy."

Like Odysseus before me, I had to rise to the challenge, my challenge being to make it back safely with my children to the Isle of Long. We registered at the front desk of the hotel next to the airport. I glanced around to see if this hotel had a star rating. We were coming from a stay in a four star hotel that was a Super Nova in the hotel rating system. Given the straits we were in, a single hotel star would have sufficed. I soon learned we had found our way to the hotel galaxy's equivalent of a Black Hole: the pool was green, the carpeting in our room worn and tattered with a burn mark of an iron where someone had ironed clothes on the floor.

There were disturbing sounds, which I didn't want to explain, coming through the paper thin walls of the rooms around us. The hotel boasted an hourly rate that attracted the seductive sirens.

"Mom, that lady must be very religious; she keeps saying 'Oh God' and 'Jesus Christ.'"

I replied, "She's praying for the second coming."

"What do you mean, Mom?"

"Never mind," I said, trying to ignore the sound of the headboard of the bed in the adjoining room banging against the wall.

Before we went to bed, I moved a dresser in front of the door for safety and slept with both kids in the bed with me. I was afraid a Cyclops might find its way into our room. The next day at the complimentary buffet, I picked up a plate from the table and a cockroach scurried out. I pointed this out to the waitress who replied, "That's Florida for you," and went about her business without removing the plate.

We flew out in the afternoon and were picked up at the airport by Nick, who had already been to the airport the day before to collect our luggage. I don't know why he was so annoyed. Odysseus was gone for ten years. I was only one day late. Putting aside the return flight mishap, all said and done, we had a great time in Florida and at least my children and I could say we had been to Disney World.

I was on a roll. There were so many experiences that I wanted to give Ian and Rhea. When I was growing up, my Auntie Annie was the cultured one in the family. I believe it was a picture of her, standing at a railroad station wearing a suit, which inspired me to become a professional. I didn't know what I wanted to be but I knew I wanted to look like that person. Auntie Annie feared that I would get no exposure to proper culture. She took it upon herself to give me the basics, taking me to a Broadway show, a ballet, an opera, and a fancy restaurant. She was the one who answered my troubled questions about why the male ballet dancers wore tights and had bulges at their groins. I think she said it was their "anatomy."

I followed my aunt's lead with my own children and ventured out of suburbia to take them to shows in Manhattan. One was the Radio City Music Hall Easter extravaganza during which the Rockettes, dressed in flowing white gowns, formed a funeral processional placing white lilies on the center stage. Knowing that my children had not grown up in a strictly Christian tradition, I should have provided them with some context. Rhea's voice rang out throughout the theater when she asked, "Who died?" I answered Rhea in a more discreet whisper, "Jesus Christ died. I'll explain later." There were so many snickers in the audience that I was afraid the Rockettes would lose their concentration and fall over one another like stacked dominos.

Another time I planned a big New York excursion that included a train ride into Manhattan, a nice lunch, a visit to a souvenir shop, and the main event, the Broadway show Cats at the Winter Garden Theater. Rhea tripped and noted, with full dramatic delivery, that she had "fallen down on Broadway." We returned home after a very long day and Ian asked if we could go into my office across from the train station. He adored playing with my stapler and paper clips. The photocopy machine was over the top. When I told him it was too late, he said, "If I had known we weren't going to stop at your office, I would never have agreed to go today!" I admit to getting a bit theatrical myself and hitting him on the head with the Playbill. That's two strikes against me: the windbreaker walloping and the Playbill pummeling. My nomination for the Herald's Mother of the Year would have to wait.

We went to the circus, the Planetarium, and some of Nick's favorite haunts: zoos, aquariums, and, especially, botanical gardens. Walking through a tropical rain forest with snow on the ground outside was a great way to spend a Sunday afternoon. If we couldn't afford a trip to the Amazon or an African safari, the Bronx Botanical Gardens or Zoo were the next best things. I found a name for what I did as a parent when I was watching a show on television about the largest aquarium in the world, in Valencia, Spain. The aquarium caretakers provided

"environmental stimulation" to the Beluga whales.

I had no interest in staying home and being domestic. My desk was a mess with mail piled high. I pulled out the bills to make sure they were paid but everything else was given cursory attention.

Baking cookies or a cake was something I would leave to our house-keeper, Connie. I knew how to sew, but my skills were as rusty as the unused sewing machine that had been submerged under water in the furnace room during a flood from the canal. The machine was a gift from my mother when I left home to live with Nick. Whether I ever planned to sew anything or not, it was the kind of gift a mother used to give to a daughter.

My mother recalled how, when I was twelve years old, I sewed my own clothing. I took Home Economics and learned how to make a wrap-around skirt with everyone else, but I had more motivation than my classmates did to develop my skills further. The austerity Loom of Life of my childhood was not able to provide me with cloth-ing that reflected the image I wanted to project as a pre-teen. My cousin, who had curves that my body didn't know about, gave me hand-me-downs and the pants hung ridiculously on my frame. My mother told me they fit perfectly fine, but I taught myself to make my own pants, matching plaid at the seams and tapering them to the exact fit I wanted. Necessity had been the mother of invention, and lacking a current necessity, the sewing machine was in disuse and disrepair.

One of the advantages of joint parenting is that each person contributes his or her talents to the family. I don't know how things operate and Nick does. I define technology expansively as "a process which uses electricity or a battery." After living in the same house for twenty-five years, I still didn't know which switches control which out-door lights. I have driven around in my car, after the semi-annual time changes for Daylight Savings, with the clock showing an hour later than it is because I didn't know how to change it. I just waited until we had to advance the clocks ahead an hour in the spring so that the time would be correctly set again; it was only wrong half of the year.

A favorite scene from the movie <u>City Slickers</u> has two of the urban cowboys riding with the herd and one is trying to explain to the other how to program a VCR. As technology is evolving so quickly, by the time I learn one technology, it becomes obsolete. When I was growing up, computers occupied entire rooms. I could not have envisioned my future household with four personal computers and smart phones that function as hand held computers and cameras. I stopped on the street to take a beautiful photograph with my phone, but all I got was a yellow screen. I gave up on the photo and worked a bit on changing my settings. When I arrived home, I saw that I had stuck a yellow post-it with a phone number on the back that was covering the lens. My technology challenges continue to the present, no matter what the instrument.

I was peer pressured into learning to text because "All of my friends' mothers know how to text" and I opened a Facebook account after my mother began posting on FB! In addition to being techno-Amish, I am sport stupid. Rhea and Ian played on local soccer teams from the time they were each six years old. Being a Soccer Mom in our culture has become a pivotal role in modern family life. As much as I loved the sport of soccer, I never figured out "off-sides." It didn't matter. All I needed to know was whether we won or lost and to say "great job" when either child came off the field. I left it to Nick to discuss ways to improve their game.

Swimming was an important skill to teach our children, especially living on the water and going out on a boat, as often as we did. The problem was that I didn't like to put my head under water. My friend from the Philippines said they used to laugh at the American women at the hotels dog paddling around the pool with their heads out of the water. That would have been me. She and her friends swam like seals. While I couldn't teach Ian and Rhea to dive, I could take them to lessons at the local pool, and I did that every summer.

Being involved as a stage mom was more to my liking. Rhea started acting and singing with Rocco's Musical Theater before she could read or write. She went on to have several major roles in school plays and auditioned for American Idol with a great deal of support from both Nick and me. Ian was still traumatized from his daffodil yellow chicken costume and never performed again.

Nick taught our children about nature, sports, and technology. From me, they had cultural experiences, as many as I could squeeze into our time together. They benefitted from the balance of the influences that we each could provide. My "To-do List" for the first half of the '90's read: "Take kids to Disney/return safely, even if not on time," "Leave housekeeping, cooking, and technology to others" and "Give kids the most colorful tapestry of childhood possible."

The former evening's tribulations were quickly forgotten the next morning when we awoke to a gorgeous tropical day and breakfast poolside.

NINE

At the Bottom of God's Purse ...is Change

The underwear was folded in our drawers and we were all leading fulfilling lives when our housekeeper Connie was in charge of our house. Our Loom of Life operated on a balanced budget, our daily routine was within parameters we could call sane, and there was a minimal amount of struggle and strife. I arrived at the house to a home-cooked dinner, helped with homework, or taxied to activities. Essentially, my life was stable but we exist on a rotating and revolving planet of water and rock wrapped around a core of molten lava. Stability is an illusion. To establish a sense of stability, we stake out our piece of the planet and establish a home, family, and connections that tether us.

Thirteen years into my marriage, a crisis developed. The problem began when the marriage of Nick's younger like-a-twin brother broke up in a contentious divorce. Having already suffered through a very painful divorce himself, Nick began to examine and question the foundation of our relationship. He dredged up incidents from our courtship that were better off left in the past. He was on full scale emotional meltdown, and career-wise, he was experiencing extreme burn-out.

Nick had gone into teaching at age twenty-one. His independent thinking and unconventional ways were a poor match with the school district's conservative administration. He decided to retire after twenty-five years of teaching, which was nine years short of the age when he could collect his retirement benefits. Suddenly we were faced with a single income and no need or money for a full time housekeeper. After ten years of relying on Connie, we had to let her go. Connie was much more prepared for this change in circumstances than we were; she started a seamstress business from her home and we were left to weave a new cloth.

Since Nick wasn't employed and I continued to work, he was the logical choice to take over the household tasks that Connie had handled. He was comfortable with this reversal of traditional roles, which was remarkable given that his father once nailed a pair of pants to the wall in the living room and said to his mother, "I wear the pants in this house." It may have been in response to his father feeling threatened by developments in the changing society around him, as well as his own son's household. He might have thought that women's liberation was a contagion. He told his wife, "Don't get any ideas," which ironically, were the exact words he said to his own son when Nick left for college, ostensibly, to expand his mind with new ideas.

Nick approached his new household roles methodically. He printed out a shopping list that contained all of the items that we frequently bought from the supermarket. When an item was used up, we were supposed to circle it on the list. If an item was not circled, it might not be purchased, even if it was toilet paper. His food shopping style was definitely a product of his childhood experience.

When he was growing up, there were too many people in his house-hold sharing too little food. One chicken was divided eight ways; each member of the family was assigned a part, for life. The last-born siblings got the short end of that deal, wings being all that were left. Guests were offered the tail. Reacting to this scarcity consciousness, Nick couldn't leave the supermarket aisles without a cart loaded to the brim.

We had a revealing conversation about how we each view his extensive shopping and it is a lesson about how communication can sort through differences. When I circled an item on the list, Nick was likely to buy two. I asked him once why he had purchased two con-tainers of cottage cheese, knowing that it is a highly perishable item. He explained that he had noticed I finished the prior container in just a few days. That was okay with me. I moved on to eating some-thing else. In fact, I had an opposite reaction when I saw two con-tainers in the refrigerator. I checked the expiration date and thought about how much cottage cheese I was going to have to eat by that date. His purchase was out of pure consideration but my reaction was exasperation. The exchange taught me a great deal about our ingrained views.

There is a curious twist when you analyze not just the quantity of food purchased but what was bought. The only theory I could come up with is that being able to afford non-essential items, is a sign of abundance. It is all about the abundance. Half of the bottom shelf of our pantry became dedicated to marinades. There were ten choices of teas-caffeinated and herbal. Maybe as a nod to my work in immigration, we had equal opportunity rice without discrimination: Spanish, yellow, black, brown, and white. Our Mediterranean shelf harkened back to our honeymoon in Greece: canned octopus, hearts of palm, and artichokes packed in either water or oil. Nick's study of martial arts was reflected in his Asian cuisine including bamboo shoots and canned lychees. In the event of a nuclear winter or natural disaster, our family would have a difficult time surviving on the contents of our pantry. However, we would have made out well in an International Food Fair.

We soon learned from our nightly dinners that our new household chef was not comfortable with using the oven but he had lots of experience barbecuing from our annual 4th of July party that was a three grill event. Barbecuing appeals to the primal urge of man to throw a hunk of raw meet onto a fire. Grill manufacturers have capitalized on this male urge and developed super grills like the multiple burner, six and a half foot Kalamazoo. Nick's first dinners consisted of grilled meat, fish, or chicken with grilled vegetables. He found an old wok that we had never used and he branched out into stir-fry dinners.

We owned many cookbooks but they were never opened. The one time there was a cookbook out on the counter it should have tipped me off that something was amiss, but I just noted that it was unusual that he was following a recipe. When it was time to sit down for dinner, I looked at the baking dish on the table and commented that the legs didn't look like chicken legs. That was when I learned that we would be eating a rabbit that one of his patients had given him.

Even though I acknowledge that rabbit is an accepted cuisine in many cultures, I kept thinking about our pet Flemish Giant rabbit that had been a part of the family. Mr. Moustache, one of Rhea's menagerie, lived in the house with us and used the cats' litter. At night, he and Nick used to share a bag of peanuts while watching TV. Rhea and I once brought the rabbit to a mall photographer to enter him in a pet photo contest. He won in the Exotic Pet category and we have the picture of him and Rhea on her dresser; he was remembered lovingly even if cleaning up after him was not. Out of respect for our dearly departed Mr. Moustache, I boycotted the rabbit dinner.

After living in Mexico and Spain, I had become acutely aware of the animals we eat. I stopped eating meat in Mexico when confronted with an open marketplace where I had to point to the animal carcass hanging on display to request a portion of meat. There were no sanitized, clear wrapped packages in a freezer. My decision to forego animal meats was reinforced in Spain when I saw a live lamb standing in a bucket waiting to be slaughtered and later saw it hanging over the bar to be cooked and served. Today, I eat meat but with an awareness that what is on my plate once lived and breathed. I don't waste food coming from an animal. I asked Nick to eat my portion of the cooked bunny.

My ordering habits when eating out at a restaurant changed dramatically after Nick assumed the cooking responsibilities for our household. To start, I skipped over anything on the menu referred to as "grilled." My eyes would be immediately drawn to oven baked dishes such as meatloaf, pot roast, or casseroles. I salivated at the thought of ordering a side of mashed potatoes, and you had me if the dish was called "old fashioned" anything. I pined for one of Connie's meals the way I mourned the loss of southern fried chicken of my youth.

My mother learned how to cook when she was growing up in Tennessee and one of her specialties was southern fried chicken. That changed in the 1960's when studies were published on the effects of cholesterol on the human body. The chicken and biscuits in gravy were replaced with baked fish and veal stew. We had to re-set our expectations, which is always a good lesson in life and those adaptation skills had to be applied to Nick's cooking on Farmers Avenue.

As with other aspects of our relationship, Nick and I found a balance. He cooked, I cleaned. This meant that he could use every pot and utensil in the kitchen, and walk away from it when done. I don't mind the fact that clean-up is an ungratifying job that doesn't get any recognition. The tradeoff was that I walked in the door to a home-cooked dinner most nights. Had it been left to me, we would have eaten a great deal more take-out food and frozen meals.

The next chore to tackle was cleaning. Nick has a high tolerance for household dirt so it was clear to me that I could not leave this task to him. I was not a big fan of mopping and scrubbing. I preferred to work a few extra hours in my office to pay for someone else to clean. Let us each do what we are best qualified to do! I was never taught the household cleaning Hints of Heloise.

When I was growing up in Farmingdale, my mother was forced to have household help because she had a bad back that prevented her from lifting and bending. I remember soaking towels in hot water and placing them on her back to give her some relief. She hired an old woman who hailed from the south to help her. Reesie was almost as bad off as my mother was. Her hands were gnarled with arthritis. She and my mother worked together and helped each other. It was by overhearing their conversations that I learned most of my "south-ernisms" because my mother reverted to her Tennessee roots when she was around Reesie.

If Reesie dropped and broke a glass, she would say, "And I call myself helpin'." My father would come in from another room with a scowl on his face to see what happened and then just go back to whatever he was doing. My mother would say, "Don't mind him, he's a poot bloom." Heaven forbid, if he said something rude, my mother might escalate to worse than a poot bloom, a fart blossom. Then my mother would help Reesie clean up the broken glass and

Reesie would respond, "Aren't you sweetness and light?" She was. My mother was all kindness. Nick liked to remind me to be more like my mother, but it was a tall order.

Laundry was the final chore that had to be reassigned from Connie. Nick took a try at it. He washed two loads of clothing and stuffed them both in the dryer at once. Without being able to toss around, the clothing came out so wrinkled that it couldn't be ironed out. I had to re-wash everything. I accepted laundry duty. Regardless of whether or not it meant folding clothing at 11:00 at night, at least I knew my children wouldn't look like ragamuffins. I barely had time to put the laundry away. I never figured out how to fold a fitted sheet or why I had so many socks without matches. Not only wasn't the laundry folded neatly in the drawers as in the Connie era, but it was left out on top of the dryer for everyone to serve himself or herself.

I was on early morning pet patrol. The cats woke me up every day before I was ready to awaken. I tried tough love. When meowing didn't get a response, they escalated to scratching the woodwork, which almost always got a reaction from me. If I didn't respond, they progressed to the next level, jumping into a potted plant to threaten using it as kitty litter. That one got me to bolt out of bed. I staggered downstairs and cleaned out their bowls from the day before, gave them canned food, dry food, and fresh water, and then let them outside.

These were the bookends between which I stacked a full day at the office and parenting: 6:00 a.m. tending to cats and 11:00 p.m. switching laundry to dryer to fold before midnight. I write this not to portray myself as working harder than any other mom who may be reading this, but rather in solidarity knowing we all do the same and some do much more. As the saying goes, a man works from sun to sun but a woman's work is never done.

113

One night each week was dedicated to paying the bills with half of our previous resources. I became the expense slasher. All discretionary spending was up for review: subscriptions, membership, donations, or gifts. If Ian or Rhea asked me to buy some knickknack or toy, they became accustomed to the answer that we really didn't need it at this time. I didn't spend money on clothing or pampering for myself so that I could make sure my children had everything they needed and would never be embarrassed by not having money for the school trip or a present for a friend's birthday party.

When I was a young girl, about eight years old, I was at a carnival with my parents. There was a ceramic poodle, black with sparkles and a painted pink nose. I begged my mother for it. It had the huge price tag of $8.00. When I put that figure into an inflation calculator for 1960 it converts to $67 in 2017! My mother caved in and bought it for me. I made sure to adore that ceramic poodle every day to justify the extravagance. It became the Ceramic Poodle Goddess. If I had known about incense, I might have put incense burners around it and future anthropologists would have speculated about this newly discovered goddess worship.

I was responsible for balancing the budget for my family, like my mother before me and her mother before her, but when it came to holding back, we would scrimp on ourselves so that we could give something special to our children. Both of my grandmothers were role models of self-sacrifice. Grandma Sarah, my father's mother, exemplified the role of the matriarchal martyr. I wonder how people can withstand so much hardship and keep going.

Grandma Sarah was born a Jew in an area of Europe that passed back and forth between Russia and Poland. Her people were persecuted and the family sometimes had to hide in the basement until trouble passed. Once they buried all of their valuables in the backyard, so they would not be stolen by their persecutors. In the spring, they dug up the valuables and found all of their money had disintegrated.

When she was only thirteen years old, Sarah boarded a ship by herself for the United States where she had a relative. She lied and said she was sixteen. The trip to America was steward class aboard a steamship, and Sarah was one of the hardier ones who didn't get sick. She went around to others who were weak and served them herring, which was the main staple they had brought with them to eat. She became known as the "herring girl." I think that these stories that I listened to as a child must have inspired me for the work that I do as an immigration lawyer and gave me compassion towards immigrants.

When Grandma Sarah arrived in America, she found work in the garment district in sweatshops like the infamous Triangle Shirt Factory in which 146 young workers, mostly immigrants, died in 1911 due to lack of fire escapes. Sarah saved every cent she could to send money for her sister to join her. She gave the money to someone who said he was traveling to her hometown. He absconded with it and Sarah's sister not only never made it to America, she didn't survive the Holocaust. Many other members of their family also perished. Hearing this so upset me that I established a general rule of avoiding reading or watching anything related to the Holocaust. I did visit a concentration camp when I spent the summer in Germany because I felt I owed it to my heritage to go.

I remember in one of my favorite movies, Annie Hall, the namesake protagonist was getting to know Alvy Singer, played by Woody Allen. Annie recounted that her grandmother used to go to the Swap Shop and find treasures. Alvy, who was what Annie's grandmother would have called a "real Jew," captured their cultural differences by explaining that his grandmother had been too busy being raped by Cossacks to go to the Swap Shop. The scene resonated with me because of my parents' cultural collision, as well as the history I knew of my grandmother's life. My grandmother Sarah never could get used to living a comfortable lifestyle. When she sat down at a table with a tablecloth, she folded the tablecloth back and put her plate on the bare table.

My mother's mother, Annie Belle, was also a hardy, no-nonsense woman. While Sarah learned to survive in the ethnic ghettos of Brooklyn, Annie Belle raised her family on a farm outside of Nashville. She had a great deal of folk wisdom. For example, she told my mother that she should have a good breakfast of eggs because they "stick to your bones." I thought of that when I read The South Beach Diet. The author, a cardiologist, explained the glycemic index, which measures the speed at which food is converted to blood sugar. Eggs are recommended on the diet because they convert to sugar slowly thereby sustaining a feeling of being sated or, as my grandmother would say, "sticking to your bones." Folk wisdom validated.

Annie Belle had to gather firewood and clean and pluck chickens. Both of my grandmothers had to feed families of four children during the Depression with almost no money. My mother told me that she and her siblings used to fight over the one piece of pork in the can of pork n' beans. It wasn't because of hunger since the farm provided them with food. It was more to do with the fact that there were four of them and that one piece of pork became a prize.

Women are biologically pre-disposed to handle this struggle and adversity. After all, we suffer from menstrual cramps and bleed every month for nearly a week but take it in stride. I wonder how a man would hold up if he had a period for even one cycle. Try for one second picturing your significant other changing a tampon. We have a nine-month gestation and then endure the pain of childbirth. Men may have physical prowess, but women are definitely designed for withstanding pain, discomfort, and hardship.

Whenever I experienced even a moment of self-pity that my lifestyle had been turned upside down, I remembered my grandmothers and felt ridiculous. They struggled to make ends meet in a subsistence existence while I only had to adjust to the demise of our lifestyle. My problems didn't compare with what my grandmothers endured on the Richter Scale of Hardship. 1993 "To-do List:" "Stop whining and get busy fixing it!"

Our new household chef was not comfortable with using
the oven but he had lots of experience barbecuing from our
annual 4th of July party that was a three grill event.

PART TWO

TEN

Needles or Nothing

We have reached the halfway point in my story. If you haven't already done so, pull up a chair and please pour yourself a glass of wine.

The book Who Moved My Cheese? sold 26 million copies with the simple motivational fable of two mice and two little people who approach change differently. For a decade, Nick and I had taken our "cheese" for granted. Now we could either wallow in the unfairness of it all like the characters Hem and Haw or put on our sneakers and seek new cheese like the enterprising Sniff and Scurry. The lesson is that movement in a new direction helps you find new cheese. Nick's rug had been pulled out from under him. He couldn't sleep and paced around the house during the night. It was important for him to get a new direction. He decided to go back to school to train for a second career, choosing Massage Therapy.

The deadline to apply for the fall semester was approaching and Nick became overwhelmed with fear about trying something new. He claimed to not know where his diplomas and transcripts were, but I located them for him. He had always been a person who sought security: lived in the same town where he grew up, had the same job for twenty-five years, and the same house for an equal length of time. Suddenly, Nick was faced with venturing into uncharted waters and there were no life preservers on the boat. I sat him down at the table and helped him fill out the application. He submitted it on time and was accepted to study. We added tuition bills to our overhead and needed additional childcare while Nick was in school and I was at work. My mother stepped up to the plate and watched Ian and Rhea every Saturday.

Meanwhile, I was scrambling to find a way to double my income. Business had been slow. I received a feeler from a well-established attorney, Ed, who wanted to form a partnership with an eye on retiring two years down the line. I met with Ed and decided to move my practice from Rockville Centre, the town where it had been for twelve years, to the Village of Hempstead where he practiced. Drastic actions were necessary.

Rockville Centre ranks high on the list of per capita incomes in New York State. Its central landmark is a large cathedral and there is a restaurant on every block. Hempstead, my new office location, is a village that attracts a large immigrant population and has a transportation hub, making it an ideal location for an immigration practice. Not too long after I moved my office, I walked to the donut shop around the corner to get a cup of tea. I was in the habit of smiling as a matter of general principle. A woman coming towards me from the opposite direction asked, "What are you smiling about, Bitch?" I jotted a note to self, "In Hempstead, smiling may evoke hostility."

I felt displaced moving into Ed's office and adopting his office procedures. I went from a short ride to an upscale village to a parkway commute to an economically depressed area. In my office, I had to develop my own personal space heat shields to avoid mental and emotional meltdown. Re-entry into the family atmosphere necessitated a critical mood adjustment. Nick said he could feel my energy a mile and a half away when I exited the parkway on my way home. That started my routine of having a cocktail when I walked through the door. Add chips and dip and it was my own personal Happy Hour. I was much more pleasant to interact with after the mood adjustment.

Ed invited Nick and me to go out to dinner with him and his wife. This is a normal formality in the business world. Women have always had to be the business spouse to reflect well on their husbands. Ed's wife talked about how wonderful her life has been, and that if she had to marry all over again, she wouldn't change a thing. Nick had a few drinks too many and also spoke from the bottom of his heart when he replied, "Relationships suck!" Nobody can deny that relationships sometimes do suck and I know Nick was wrestling with very challenging issues. One thing was clear: the business spouse role had never been modeled for him.

When I shared this role reversal with a group, I was amazed to find that four out of five of us had been the major breadwinners in our families at one point or another. In all four families, the husbands made major career moves in their mid-forties, when they became dissatisfied in their jobs. It sounded a lot like mid-life course corrections. One spouse quit his full time work and took a part time position, one went to law school, one gave up his ministry for secular work, and my husband studied to become a massage therapist.

As much as Nick enjoyed learning to be a message therapist, to say that there were times when he was miserable with his life's upheaval would minimize the reality. Had we known about the reality television show <u>Survivor</u> at the time, we would have voted Nick off the island. Rhea and I were shopping one afternoon and saw a wood knob to use for giving massages called "The Happy

Massager." Rhea said, "Look, Mom, we could buy that for Daddy to use in school." I replied, "We would have to change the name to 'The Unhappy Massager.'"

My marriage was hanging by a thread, with financial pressures and disillusion threatening to snap it. We were both strong-willed and had terrible shouting matches. Sometimes, I would pass a real estate agency on the way home and wistfully fantasize about getting my own place. I thought how we would divide the childcare responsibilities and settle our assets, but those were idle musings because walking out of the relationship was not an option I was really prepared to take, no matter how much it "sucked." We had the complicated interdependent weaves of home and family. I felt fairly certain that my children wanted the family to stay together and I did my best to make that my foremost consideration. I have seen divorce tear apart families and the children suffer the most. I don't advocate staying in an abusive relationship, but in a relationship that could be turned around, I chose to find a way to make it work.

For the second time in my relationship with Nick, I decided to get individual counseling. His behavior crossed the line of annoying and challenging to intolerable. To my initial session, I brought a Christmas card photo of our family and said, "I want to be the family represented in this picture, not the dysfunctional family behind the façade." The counselor asked many probing questions about what I considered our family's dysfunction. One of her lines of inquiry involved what kind of discipline we used with the children. I told her about the time-out seat on the bottom step, the collection cup for quarters each time one of the children cursed, and Nick's specialty, pressure points that were sort of like a Vulcan Death Grip. The therapist was not pleased with Karate techniques being used by a black belt on our children to gain their compliance. She acted as if I had told her that my husband was disciplining our children with a cattle prod and I was standing by without stopping him.

When my mother used to get angry with my brother and me, she applied what she called "Indian burns" to our forearms. I wasn't sure whether anyone else would know what an Indian Burn is and I am fairly certain it is a politically incorrect term but I looked it up on the on-line encyclopedia, Wikipedia. To my surprise, they gave an explanation: an Indian burn is produced by grabbing a person's forearm with two hands, each one twisting the skin in the opposite direction. Like pressure points, my mother only had to apply an Indian burn once or twice and, after that, the threat was effective enough.

I was at a Comedy Club Open Microphone Night that should have been called "Stand-up Comedy as Therapy". The comedian began to rant about how his six-foot tall, blonde mother used to grab her children by the clothes with one hand and swat at them with the other. The six-foot tall blonde mother was in the audience laughing. Corporal punishment is unenlightened but more common than most families will admit, unless they have a child who reveals all as a comedian (or as an author). When it is a well-intended-though-exasperated form of discipline, it can be forgiven and apparently laughed about in retrospect. A mother's wrath is often more laughable than a father's as I learned from tales of friends who were chased by their mothers with wooden spoons or my own grandmother, who lived on a farm, and would tell her children to "Come in and bring a switch off the tree with you."

In Trevor Noah's memoir, Born a Crime, he recalls how, when he was growing up in South Africa, his mother routinely gave him a "hiding" to discipline him. He was a very mischievous child and he understood those beatings to be out of a sense of love and an attempt to guide him in the way her culture dictated. Trevor contrasted this with the violent beatings from his stepfather that had more to do with the stepfather's inner anger and frustrations than a desire to guide his stepson.

Before I leave the topic of discipline, my mother had another weapon of punishment, the silent treatment. This tactic of withholding love can be more devastating than an Indian burn, a wooden spoon to the butt, or a pressure point. At times, a person may need to ask for time to cool down, knowing that anything said in the heat of that moment might be less than kind, but eventually words are needed to express what has gone wrong and how it can be righted. My father gave the dirty look. It's best to avoid these non-verbal signs of anger because they stand in the way of meaningful conversation. In my case, it led to responding with (surprise) tears because I didn't know how to express my feelings in words. We need to learn how to express ourselves with non-violent communication, something that can take a lifetime to learn.

Eventually, Nick's mood lightened and he became intrigued with acupuncture and Chinese medicine. He obtained a license in acupuncture in addition to massage therapy. He completed a Master's degree in Chinese Medicine and embraced his new career. We adapted our house to create an office for his healing practice. Like Robert Frost's two roads diverging in a wood, in the foyer entrance of our house, we created a choice of two doors, one leading to our residence and the other being the road less traveled. Passing through it, the traveler would enter an alternative environment of new age music, incense, and screens where Nick could treat his patients with massage, acupuncture, and Chinese medicine.

The practice, which he named Martial and Healing Arts, emphasized healing but had a martial arts component. Nick embraced a new routine of starting every day by performing Tai Chi. He chose to practice in the driveway, to the chagrin of Ian and Rhea who lived in mortal fear of a friend catching him doing push-hands and elbow-strokes in front of the house. To make matters worse, if it was chilly out, he kept warm wearing a Kung Fu jacket. Nick offered to give me Martial Arts lessons, but I would be expected to bow to him and that was out of the question. Besides, it was bad enough that *he* was doing martial arts in our driveway. I didn't want us to be *that couple* that does Tai Chi together in their front yard.

Our household medicine chest was suddenly stocked with products such as Bi Yan Pian and Gui Pi Wan. Rhea didn't buy into alternative medicine back then. She kept contraband over-the-counter medications hidden in her room. Spotting a bottle in her room, my husband would say that he was woefully disappointed, as if she had been caught storing hashish in her closet instead of acetaminophen. He always suspected the harm these painkillers could cause the body and recent studies show that he was right about potential high blood pressure and liver damage from regular use. It took all of my persuasive powers to convince Nick that we could give a note to the school stating our child was returning from an absence due to a cold, even if he were sure it was due to liver chi stagnation.

The holistic health care didn't stop at needles and herbs. Nick also used a substance called Moxa to burn over an injury, directing the heat inward to the afflicted area. It smelled curiously like marijuana. The house was filled with the smell of Moxa drifting in from Nick's office and escaping out the greenhouse vent when the doorbell rang and I answered it to find my neighbor, a police officer.

"Hello! What can I do for you?"

"My son's ball went into your backyard. I just wanted to let you know I'm going back there to get it." I noticed he kept sniffing and his eyebrows were knitted into a uni-brow. I suspected the ball was a pretext to check out the smell wafting from the green house vent.

"I know what you must be thinking. It's called Moxa, spelled M-O-X-A. You can look it up. Nick is treating a patient. Your children are not going to get a contact high from it."

I sometimes agreed to take the big step through the portal labeled "Office" to be treated by Nick for a health concern. He told me I was his worst patient. I negotiated with him to treat me with massage therapy instead of acupuncture, since he is licensed to do both, but he told me it's "needles or nothing." It was hard to draw the line between the spouse and the healer. I was so used to saying, "The garbage needs to be taken out now" that I found myself saying, "The needles need to be taken out now."

"So, you want to tell me how to do acupuncture, too?" he would ask.

I married an Irish-Greek man from Long Island and found myself living with Martial and Healing Arts. Nick developed a passion for collecting Buddha statuettes: young or old, laughing or meditating, made of wood, ceramic, or glass, it didn't matter. Once people see you have a collection, they think they know the ideal gift to give and the collection grows exponentially. I complained to my friend, Jan, that we had to be the only tourists to go to New Orleans and return with a Buddha instead of Mardi Gras beads. She said to me, "A man can never have too many Buddhas!" At last count, there were twenty placed around his office on shelves, in potted plants, in his greenhouse, and on his desk.

Nick often points out that he doesn't carouse, womanize, drink, or beat me. Sure it could be worse; all he does is try my patience. On one occasion, I received a panicked telephone call because his Ninja

Stars had disappeared from the garage, and he was sure that someone had stolen them. I suggested that, since I hadn't seen any Ninjas lurking about the neighborhood, they were more than likely misplaced. Marriage is about making a relationship work despite each other's differences. I can state that living with Martial and Healing Arts has been the road less traveled.

The transition from teaching science to practicing Martial and Healing Arts took five years of education and licensing and several more years to become profitable. Nick had a new career and a home office. During that time, I was able to rally my law practice into a lucrative business. Despite not getting off to the best start with my first business dinner, the new partnership worked out well. I came to appreciate the character of Hempstead including the historic church, Clock Tower on the Town Hall, and the diversity of its population.

Nick didn't take for granted what I had done to step in and save the day. We had found "new cheese." On our twentieth wedding anniversary, he surprised me with a gift. To understand just how special this gift was, Nick is not known for his acknowledgment of special occasions. He keeps a stock of cards for each recurring holiday: birthday, anniversary, Mother's Day. When the day rolls around, he writes the current year on it and puts the recycled card on the dining room table (often after I remind him of the occasion). The cards have actually taken on sentimental value as the years accumulate. The anniversary card purchased in the 70's shows a young couple holding hands in a meadow. I like to comment that it looks just like us, if time had stood still. We can be sure that he never gets caught without a card.

One Mother's Day, I bought the gift that I wanted to receive and gave it to him in the shopping bag with a gift bag and colorful tissue paper inside for him to use. When Mother's Day rolled around, I reminded him that he had a gift for me in his closet and he took out the shopping bag and handed it to me with the tags still on the clothing, receipt in the bag, and the unused gift bag and tissue paper. I asked him if he thought he should have wrapped it to which he replied that he was never much for wrapping gifts. I should have learned this early in our relationship when I tried to interest him in romance by putting on a negligee. He would say, "Why bother with the wrapping when I only want the merchandise?"

In 1999, twenty years after our wedding, Nick gave me the diamond ring that I didn't ask for when we got engaged. It wasn't wrapped, but no matter. Though I had commented that the young gals in my office all had beautiful engagement rings, I never thought I would get one at this stage in our relationship. I told Rhea, I finally had one of "the white ones" on my hand. My "To-do List" led off with "Pull family through crisis" followed by "Wear new diamond ring." We began this chapter sitting down to have a drink, so let me raise my glass to that.

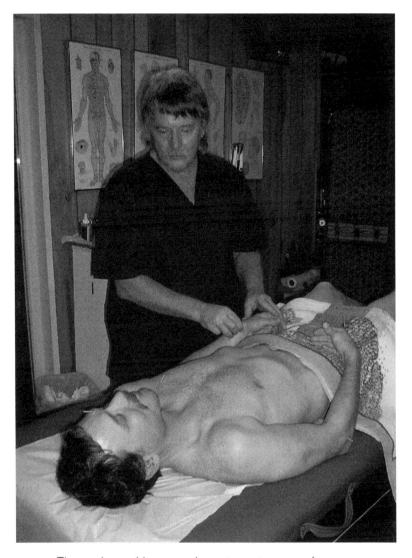

The traveler would enter an alternative environment of new age
music, incense, and screens where Nick could treat his patients
with massage, acupuncture, and Chinese medicine.

ELEVEN

The Barf Clause in the Limo Contract

Have you ever heard someone say, "I was in labor for eighteen hours and gave birth naturally to an infant with a head the size of a cantaloupe but it was all worth it because I knew one day I would have a teenager?" You haven't? That's because it has never been said. One mother of an adorable, curly haired boy clinging to her leg asked me, "How do you deal with it when they get older and aren't as cute anymore?" Her question brought to mind the short rhyme of Ogden Nash in "The Cat" which laments that, a kitten will become a cat. I tried not to be insulted on behalf of my own two kiddies, but really, what parent wants to think of their child experimenting with smoking, drinking, and liaisons with the opposite sex?

We work our way gradually into the roles. I remember when the children were babies, if somebody wanted to speak to me about teething I would say, "I'm not up to that yet, I'm still weaning from my breast." It was all on a need-to-know basis. There is nothing to prepare a woman for caring for a baby, a child, and definitely not a teen. My best advice is to develop lines of honest communication early on, and lay a foundation for the future when it is going to be critical.

I have been privy to observing some very terrible parenting in my office. When parents threaten their misbehaving children by telling them that the lawyer is going to have them arrested or some other inane lie, I wonder how that child can ever trust anything his or her parent says if this is what passes for communication. I even went so far as to question the propriety, when the children were little, of advancing the make-believe fantasies of Santa Claus, the Easter Bunny, and the Tooth Fairy, fearing it would undermine trust when they learned the truth.

Having been raised in a Jewish household, I was uncomfortable when Nick said we should tell our children that there is a Santa Claus and an Easter Bunny, but I played along. When we tell a fib, we all know that to maintain it often requires a complex web of untruths. For example, if your child believes in Santa Claus, the question always arises as to why there is more than one Santa Claus at the mall or why this Santa looks different than the last one we saw. So then we have to explain how Santa has many helpers because he can't be everywhere at once. "How does he choose his helpers?" and "Can I be one?" If you have inquisitive kids, it can be unnerving. When asked how the Easter Bunny knows where all the little boys and girls live to deliver their baskets, I said they must have some kind of Bunny Directory called "Hop and Stop."

I was raised with the Tooth Fairy, so I didn't have as much difficulty with that white lie. One time, I was already in bed when I remembered Ian had lost a tooth. I got up and went to my pocketbook in the dark to get a one-dollar bill to place under his pillow. The next day, Ian ran into our bedroom with great excitement to tell us that the Tooth Fairy had left him ten dollars. I considered, even if for only a brief moment, concocting a complex story about how the Tooth Fairy sometimes doesn't have change and relies upon the parents to leave it for her the next day, because she really only meant to give a dollar.

These innocent make-believe fantasies aside, I have tried to shoot from the hip knowing the stakes were going to get higher. It comes as a shock to all of us when our children hit puberty and become interested in the opposite sex and, conversely, the opposite sex in them. I remember walking through the mall and thinking it had been a while since so many men had stared at me. Was it my new hairstyle or the fact that I had taken off some weight? That's when it hit me . . . they were looking at my daughter, not me! When her braces came off and the baby fat re-aligned itself into feminine curves, she became quite lovely.

When a mother has this epiphany, she can hope it is not too late to give "the talk". Timing is everything. If it is too late, you will know by the rolling of the eyes and, if it is too soon, by the vacant stare. Many parents leave it to the school to give the "girls in the auditorium/boys in the gym" talk. At a retreat I attended, several women had the same experience of being handed a booklet on sex and being told, "Ask me if you have any questions." Of course, their parents relied upon the fact that there would be no questions, or if there were any, their children's peers would answer them. I remember trying to get my brother to explain to me what "69" was. He said, "Look at the numbers and think of the circles in the numbers as being heads." I drew eyes and smiles on the circles to help me visualize but I was still clueless.

My favorite source of information, the morning radio show, cited a study in which it was found that the average age for girls today to lose their virginity is 15, while for their mother's generation, it was 19. When Rhea told me she had fallen in love and could see herself becoming sexually involved with her boyfriend, the next step was to set up an appointment for my daughter with a gynecologist. Pregnancy was a far greater harm in my eyes than sexual activity. Of course, Nick didn't agree with my head on confrontation of the sexuality issue. He thought I was encouraging promiscuity. Au contraire.

My ideas were strongly woven by a Loom of Life experience from my childhood. My babysitter was raised by a very strict parent who had oppressive rules about what she could wear to school, whom she could date, when she had to come home, and every other aspect of her personal life. When she arrived at school, she put make-up on and hiked up her skirt. When she was babysitting, she had her boyfriend come over after we were in bed. Our babysitter became pregnant while in high school. I would hate to think this happened on our family couch. In those days, girls who were pregnant disappeared for several months and came home without the baby, presumably given up for adoption. It was a huge stigma. I realized that all of her father's rules didn't stop her from being sexually active and encouraged her to act rebelliously.

In order to keep an open dialogue, it has to be as non-judgmental as possible. Some might say that I relinquished my parental role by not imposing my judgments, but the way I saw it, I knew a great deal about what was happening in my children's worlds, which sometimes was more of a heavy burden than a cop-out. For Rhea's prom, she organized the limousine and collected the money but couldn't sign the contract because she was under eighteen. I signed it and became aware of the "barf clause" wherein any person vomiting in the limo would cause a clean-up surcharge to be imposed.

At a graduation party several days later, I joked with one of the parents that her daughter had invoked the barf clause. The mother bristled and demanded an explanation from her daughter. The daughter looked wide-eyed at her mother and said that she had tasted some vodka, hated it and spit it out causing the driver to *think* she was throwing up and unfairly charge them all for cleaning. When her mother was satisfied with this explanation, I walked away in amazement.

In High School, Rhea was the more challenging child. A group of hoodlums crashed her seventeenth birthday party and set our lawn furniture on fire when we wouldn't let them come in. Would anyone give birth knowing that this was where child rearing was headed? We didn't escape rebellion from Ian-he just saved it for college. In high school, he was concentrated on three sports and honor grades, but this had its own challenges. In eleventh grade, he admonished me saying that "real mothers" were already investigating colleges and taking their children to visit them. I was wounded to the core.

I asked around and learned that my former partner, Margie, was one of those "prime time mothers" who was finding out what AP subjects were best for her son to take so that he could be accepted into the university of his choice. She was sending him to visit potential universities on weekends in his junior year and she couldn't believe that I didn't have a list of schools that Ian was considering. I became concerned enough to call his guidance counselor and find out if we really were lagging. She reassured me that the school would lead us (me) through the application process when it was time, and I knew that whatever I needed to do, I would figure out.

I wore the hats of Editor-In-Chief of all essays leaving the house, Tester-of-SAT-Vocabulary-Words, and Tutor-of–Spanish-Verb-Conjugations. Helping Ian and Rhea with Spanish was frustrating for all concerned because I was supposed to be an expert. I was a Spanish major in college and owned a bi-lingual law practice. The reality was that I studied Spanish literature in the early 1970's and I explained legal concepts to Central American clients. Neither of these prepared me for a dialogue entitled, "At the Beach." If I didn't know what "bronceadora" was (sun tan lotion) I would be met with a disparaging "I thought you were fluent in Spanish!" I never had to explain to my clients about wearing sun tan lotion, and it didn't come up while reading the epic, <u>Don Quixote</u>.

Children think you have all the answers, which we all know we don't. Rhea, always the inquisitive one, asked how nouns were assigned gender in Spanish. Who decided that bread is masculine (*el* pan) and butter is feminine (*la* mantequilla)? Was there a council on noun gender when the language was emerging? Today, with the exploration of sexual fluidity, I can imagine a conversation of the noun "bread" telling his shrink that he was assigned a male gender but identifies as a female noun.

When it came time to take Ian and Rhea out in the car to learn to drive, I was the designated Driver Education Instructor. It was completely under protest that I became the clenched fist, white knuckled parent pressing the invisible brakes on the passenger side of the car. People talk of the terrible two's, but terrible teens can be worse when you compare potty training to teaching your teen to merge onto a parkway at fifty-five miles per hour. Potty training is not life threatening.

All of this multi-tasking has an anthropological root. From the time that woman began to walk upright, she had to tend to the daily tasks of survival, like gathering food or stoking the fire, while having an infant on her hip and a toddler hanging from her leg. Looking back at my roles as a mother, I marvel at how many ill-fitting hats I have worn. I even had a stint as Sunday school teacher when Ian and Rhea attended religious education at our congregation. In one of my lessons, I invited the class to bring in contemporary music with religious references. Ian brought "Counting Blue Cars" by Dishwalla that refers to God in the feminine gender, and the child in the song wants to ask Her why we are who we are. The gender reference was fully discussed. When either Ian or I hears that song played, we always reach out to each other.

When Ian joined the wrestling team, I became the reluctant Wrestling Mom. I found that wrestling was hard to watch as my son's leg or arm was being locked into an impossible position. My motherly nature wanted to protect my child, not see him get hurt. I made it to some of the matches but deferred to Nick as the regular rooting parent. Ian wrestled in the lower weight classes and, during the season, he looked like the poster child for a campaign to rid the world of famine. For one whole week before a major tournament, he went to sleep wearing a plastic trash bag over his sweat suit to sweat out those extra drops of water weight.

Nick came from a wrestling family. His father was chosen for the U.S. Olympic team in 1936 but he couldn't afford the training and travel. Nick's own picture hung on the wall of fame at his high school and he was a state champ in college. He attends wrestling reunions fifty years after his last match where his fellow combatants reminisce about every take down, pin, and unfair call that has replayed in their minds for decades. Later in life, Nick was inducted into the National Wrestling Hall of Fame. Given this legacy, he was one hundred per cent behind all of Ian's wrestling routines. I was proud of Ian for his spirit, discipline, and leadership in becoming team captain, but it was a nerve-wracking sport. We always had a first aid ice pack ready to use in the freezer.

To keep my energy positive and not lose myself to all of the commotion around me, I turned to meditation, prayer, and uplifting self-help books including the familiar writings of my old friend, Wayne Dyer. I went to see Wayne whenever he spoke in New York City and we always shared a heart-felt hug. I sent him holiday greeting cards and he sent me motivational tapes and signed my books. In a letter he wrote to me in 1984, he reminisced that I gave him the room that launched his speaking career, referring to that school auditorium on Main Street in Port Washington. I began to read Wayne's work, <u>Real Magic</u>, which encouraged me to discard limits I placed on myself and manifest my life's purpose. In my absorption of the needs of my family, I had forgotten I had a life's purpose.

My creative energy was tapped and I decided that it was time for me to join the show as a performer, rather than its ringmaster. I became driven by the idea of writing a novel about one of my client's experiences that had a stranger-than-fiction plot. We met for several weeks during which I taped as she told me the details of her life. I researched background information about her native Russia. Then I was ready to put it down on paper. When I told my mother I was planning to write a novel, she suggested I might start with a short story, but my mind was set.

My first bare bones draft was one hundred pages and I proudly gave it to the protagonist to read the product of our collaboration. She shook her head and said with her "r's" trilling, "This reads like one hundred page affidavit." She talked to me about the great Russian novels and how the writers painted pictures with their words. I was devastated to find out that being able to write an article for the "Nassau Lawyer" didn't mean I could write a novel. I registered for writing classes at local colleges and attended seminars to learn a new way of expressing myself.

Sundays were my laundry and writing days. I created plots, developed characters, and invented dialogues in between sorting darks from whites and trying to match clean socks; always an odd number. (By the way, I uncovered the conspiracy when I found an unmatched sock in the corner of a fitted sheet that I was struggling to fold). Three manuscripts and hundreds of laundry loads later, I decided to publish a book about a Salvadoran man separated from his family. The book, in many ways, captured the heart and soul of my work as an immigration lawyer. Like the humble man in the song "Guantanamera," I reached a point in my life where I could also say, that before I die, that I wanted to release the verses from my soul. The words poured into my head and had to be put on paper. I found myself scribbling notes on a train ride or in my car in a parking lot.

Wayne Dyer gave me a strong endorsement letter to help me advance the book. In his words, it was "all green lights" to go full speed ahead but finding an agent or a publisher turned out to be a no-go speed bump. I decided to self-publish. A friend, who was a graphic artist, designed the book and contracted for its printing. The promotion of my novel was up to me. I began speaking at local churches and community groups about the need for the continuing contributions of immigrants to our country and the hardships they endure to make a life here. I had never enjoyed public speaking. Going back to my law school days, I dreaded being called upon to brief a case orally in a large lecture hall.

Comedian Jerry Seinfeld observed that the fear of dying is rated as people's number two fear, while public speaking is number one. This leads one to the logical conclusion that it is preferable to be the one in the coffin than the one giving the eulogy. For women, the fear of speaking is compounded by a history of not being allowed to speak. In the 1600's outspoken women were labeled witches. In the 1800's when women were speaking out against slavery and for suffrage rights, they were called disgraceful harlots. The negative attitude towards women speaking in public persisted up until the second women's liberation movement of the nineteen sixties. Former British Prime Minister Margaret Thatcher reportedly took voice lessons to remove some of the more female pitches and inflections that were a part of her natural speech patterns. There was not much of a female orator model.

I was petrified when my aunt arranged for me to be a speaker at the Brandeis Women's Author luncheon, where over one hundred fifty women would attend. Rhea had just played the lead role of Nellie Forbush in <u>South Pacific</u> at her high school. If she could sing, dance, and kiss in front of several hundred people, I thought I should be able to pull off this luncheon talk. Rhea came with me to give encouragement. As the women began to arrive, I noticed that almost all were elderly. Rhea leaned over to me and whispered, "Mom, if they can hear you, they'll love you!" I made it through that speaking engagement and future ones became easier.

While relying upon juggling skills to rival any circus act and exploring my own creativity, I guided both kids through high school. My "To-do List" for the latter 1990's: "Walk tightrope of raising teens without a safety net while swinging overhead on a trapeze of creative energy."

While relying upon juggling skills to rival any circus act and exploring my own creativity, I guided both kids through high school.

TWELVE

Adult Rated
Shopping List

The new millennium arrived and it was time for us to launch our first born out from the home where he was raised since birth. Tulane University in New Orleans offered Ian an academic scholarship to attend college. He and I flew down to Louisiana to visit the campus. I remember my first impression of New Orleans. The oak trees arched over the road, a trolley car rode down the middle, and Cajun restaurants with outdoor dining flanked either side. There were jazz musicians playing everywhere we went. I thought that this is not just another state, but another state of mind. Ian was equally taken with the city and the school but he had another option to consider. He had also been accepted to a special program at the University of Maryland.

"Here's your choice," I said, "a nearby, academic environment with a high professor to student ratio or a wild adventure far from home. What's it going to be, crab cakes or jambalaya?" Spicy Jambalaya prevailed; he mailed out his acceptance to Tulane in New Orleans. Comedian Colin Quinn once addressed the Tulane student body and complimented them on being the most brilliant of all of the students in the country. He reasoned that, even though the Tulane student body might not have the academic credentials of the students from Harvard and Yale, Tulane students had managed to convince their parents to send them to study in New Orleans! It was known at that time as the Big Easy.

Ian's first year in college was a chance for him to break out of the discipline he had followed for over six years in junior and senior high as a scholar athlete. By the end of his first semester at college, he was on residential and disciplinary probation, but somehow managed to keep up his grades. Then came the second semester with fraternity pledging and Mardi Gras. We think that Ian never totally returned from Mardi Gras that year. He added academic probation to the list. I remember that he told me he had aced his Calculus final when in reality he earned a D. He apparently had devised his own system of Calculus that was not the same as the one in the syllabus. One of his lowest moments was having surgery on his ear to remove the eggshell smashed in it during fraternity pledging. I fretted and feared that Ian had blown his opportunity to continue at Tulane. I hoped it was a passing phase and that he would revert to being the sensible son he had always been.

A young woman came into Ian's life and helped to settle him down, because that's what we women do. I passed the torch to his girlfriend. He stayed that summer in New Orleans, took a class and got back on the academic track. I was relieved that I didn't have to do something parental, like hauling his rear back to New York because "parental" had never been my style. That year, when we drafted our holiday newsletter, my version was scrapped: "My son pulled himself back from academic, disciplinary, and housing probation and kept his scholarship." The final edit was a more upbeat version, "Our son thoroughly enjoyed his first year in college."

145

Three years later, Rhea chose to go to the University of Miami, with a scholarship to sing in two choirs for the school. Rhea loved the Miami weather (hurricanes aside) and the tropical flora and fauna. The University had a palm tree lined lake with a fountain in the center. Alligator hunters were seen from time to time cruising the glistening surface in pursuit of alligators that took up residence there. The alligators snapping up ducks from the pond was disturbing to students and visitors alike. Of course, snapping up students would be even more troubling. Rhea and four other girls shared a five-bedroom ranch in Coral Gables, in violation of the peace and tranquility of their neighborhood. The congregants of the church across the street most definitely didn't approve of the topless sunbathing (this seems very familiar from my college days).

The university had a unique Music Business and Entertainment program with only eleven students selected to participate. The program was within the broader Bachelors in Music, which required each student to take basic piano training. Rhea was used to everything academic coming easily to her, but piano playing turned out to be her nemesis. She blamed it on short fingers and suggested that she should get a letter from a psychologist that she had "Piano Phobia" to be exempt from the proficiency test. I used the opportunity as a teachable moment to explain that facing a challenge, and even failing, would build character. She passed the proficiency test but we were never sure if she mastered the material or just earned a sympathy grade because she reportedly cried from beginning to end. Either way, she was proud of herself for facing the challenge and overcoming it.

My father was critical of the sacrifices Nick and I made to send our children to name brand colleges instead of giving them the same state university education that my brother and I received. He never missed an opportunity to expound on this topic. "After all," he says, "didn't you and your brother do well for yourselves?" Despite his philosophy on the matter, when I ran into financial trouble the year that they were both in college at once, while Ian was a senior and Rhea a freshman, to my Dad's great credit, he helped me out.

My idea was that I wanted to give my children a broader view of society by sending them away from the insular culture of Long Island and the New York State of Mind. They had both worked hard in high school and earned substantial scholarships. I wanted them to experience new places and meet people from all over the country. They were exposed to friends whose families had more financial wealth and prestigious connections. This necessarily meant that, at times, they had to deal with envy. When Ian's friends were all going to Europe for spring break and he was home on Farmers Avenue, I reminded him, "You were born with a plastic spoon, not a silver one, in your mouth" He looked at Nick doing Tai Chi in the driveway and corrected me. "I was born with wooden chopsticks in mine," he said. Not to say there is anything wrong with chopsticks. Jerry Seinfeld pointed out, in one of his routines, even though the Chinese have seen the fork they are sticking with the chopstick.

We told our children that we look forward to their supporting us when they land those great jobs after graduation. Ian read <u>Rich Dad Poor Dad</u> and told us that we exemplified the poor Dad model, highly educated but ignorant about financial matters. I would agree wholeheartedly. Nick has two Master's Degrees, but thinks an IRA Rollover is a wrestling move. I encourage our children to be savvier about finances than we are.

I believe that I qualify to write a list of top-ten calls you don't want to receive from your children away from home. "I had to have an eggshell surgically removed from my ear" would be on it, along with, "Don't worry, my friend's Dad got us a lawyer." My daughter would also contribute to the list. I had too many telephone calls from her telling me, "Call the insurance company; I had an accident."

When Rhea had her first car accident, I contacted a friend for some advice. He said, "Welcome to the club. You get used to it; I'm on my kids' third accident." It wasn't long before I was running for the accident club president. The low point was when Rhea had an accident on the way to the body shop to replace her front bumper from the previous fender bender. I was reminded of Erma Bombeck's sage warning that you should never lend a car to someone to whom you gave birth.

Once both of our children were away at college, Nick and I entered that phase of our lives commonly known as the empty nest. The depression I experienced was not immediately recognizable due to its subtlety. I began thinking that I had experienced the essence of what life had to offer: I had traveled as a single woman, earned a doctorate degree, married, raised children, developed a career, and wrote a book inspired by my career. I felt that, if my life ended at that point, I would be all right with it. In retrospect, I realize that I was in an empty nest depressive state thinking that my life ended with my children moving away.

These types of ruminations are apparently not uncommon. One friend recalls being up to his neck in wedding arrangements with his bride-to-be when his mother called to inform him that she had purchased side-by-side burial plots for herself and her husband. She may not have understood the subconscious implications of her actions but her message was clear: "Don't worry about your father and me; go on with your lives, we're almost dead anyway."

My parents modeled an opposite reaction to seeing their children and grandchildren moving on with their lives. They decided it was time to downsize the house and move into a senior living community where they rediscovered a zest for living. They were each approaching eighty years of age and it was foreseeable that they would not be able to continue the rigors of home ownership. They didn't want to impose on me with their needs. There is a saying that my mother taught me: "A son is yours until he has a wife; a daughter is yours for the rest of your life."

With my brother married, moving around the country and traveling the world, I knew that the day-to-day helping of my parents would fall upon me even though we were both dutiful children. An interesting dynamic developed with my brother's and my respective relationships with our parents. I visited most Sundays for an hour or two. When he came to visit, he stayed with them for three or four days. When he complained that they were driving him crazy, I replied, "You chose this arrangement. I can go home after my weekly visit."

After my parents moved into their new community, they became so busy with activities that they hardly had time for me. Jack and Jane were transformed into high school kids, always on their way out to a group, a party, a dance, swimming, canasta . . . the list was long. They gave up hosting holiday dinners in favor of using their oven to store bread. It was a new stage in my life as well as theirs-one which required adjustment and contributed to my empty nest loneliness. It was unsettling because my parents had been so available, living fifteen minutes away from me for twenty years. I could drive to their house if I was alone for an evening. At age fifty, it was time for me to give them their well-deserved space.

My parents made many new friends in their senior community, but they all know they are in the sunset of their lives. Many seniors object to moving into assisted living because they don't want to live with "a bunch of old people," which always sounds humorous coming from a super senior. My mother volunteered organizing pushers, which in her community, meant wheel chair pushers. You know you're associating with "a bunch of old people" when you throw a party and your guests RSVP that their "significant other" is their home attendant.

Living with "a bunch of old people" is undeniably the downside of a senior community. When the administration threw a party for the new residents, a ninety-year old man succumbed to a heart attack while dancing the polka. I suppose, if you have to choose a way to go, that would not be a bad one, although I have never been a fan of the polka. At the memorial gathering, the wheel chair pushers were pressed into service and there was a bottleneck of walkers requiring someone to direct pedestrian traffic, but that's life in the senior zone.

My mother made the observation that, when she was young, she thought all old people were nice. Then she came to realize that they run the gamut of human character with age accentuating characteristics such that people who were nice are even sweeter and those who weren't can be quite ornery. As we enter each stage in life, we find that we arrive there with the same people who have been with us all along. We hope for a bit more wisdom with age but that's not always the case.

Nick and I adjusted to life as a couple, married without children in the home. It's not all that difficult to get used to the quiet, peaceful orderliness of a home. When the children were young, I had a magnet on the refrigerator that said, "Cleaning up when there are children around is like shoveling when it is still snowing." Nick and I were now able to sit down to a pleasant, uninterrupted dinner every night. I arrived home to the aroma of a home cooked meal and the sound of classic rock in the background.

Despite a slow start as family cook, Nick became a gourmet chef, serving a healthy, delicious dinner and fussing over the "presentation" of the food. He has a photo album on Facebook of some of his gastronomical creations. We have an hour together from the time I get home from work until he starts seeing his evening patients. It's a perfect time for interaction with each other; we don't have an opportunity to take on any contentious subjects. Usually we watch the news followed by an episode of "Law and Order," or during the playing season, a baseball game. The television entertainment further limits conversation during our hour together to commercial breaks, unless the commercials are good, and then we watch them as well.

Our conversation has gone from the all night, serotonin-driven discussions of our dating days to dialogue that can fit within the time frame of boring commercials about health products and prescription drugs that are favored sponsors of the evening news. Sometimes we speak in code:

"Did you call whatshisname about the leak?"

"Yeah, he'll take care of it when he comes to fix the uh, you know . . ."

It's like a language spoken by twins. Next in this progression is a click language.

Ian and Rhea, though physically far away, kept in daily telephone contact and had plenty to talk about. At my office, my cell phone was out on the desk so the family could reach me any time during the day. Usually the calls were fairly mundane but I tolerated the interruptions because I didn't want to be the fisherman who let the big one get away. There was the time Rhea called from college while I was in consultation with a client and said, "Mom, I just figured out what I want to do with the rest of my life." I asked my client if he could excuse me for a minute.

Nick complained that I merely stretched the umbilical cords to Miami and New Orleans. He had actually cut the umbilical cord for each child under the supervision of the midwife and then spent the next twenty years trying to get me to cut it emotionally. We currently have a family group text, which is active all day. At some point, I suppose it will evolve into the once-a-week phone call but I'm not ready for that yet. Separation of children and their mothers occurs gradually, in incremental degrees.

The first day Ian was to leave for nursery school, we role-played his getting on the bus. He seemed to have it down pat, but he had not anticipated one variable. When that bus door opened up, there was a complete stranger sitting in the driver's seat. In defiance of the laws of physics, Ian leaped from the ground from a standing position and wrapped both arms and legs around me so tightly that I could barely pry myself free. The bus driver was able to convince him that he was in no harm and Ian reluctantly boarded the bus.

A year later, when Ian was in kindergarten, he surprised me on the way to the bus stop. "Kiss me good-bye here, Mommy," he said. I was about to ask why when I realized that he didn't want his friends to see me kissing him good-bye; his first act of separation. From then on, he learned separation more quickly and better than I did. The University of Miami gave the parents of freshmen a book entitled, Letting Go. They knew that the students were in for the best time of their lives and it was the parents who were at home wringing their hands with worry.

Perhaps you have heard the phrase "helicopter parent". One of my feedback group members works at a university told me that this is what universities call parents who hover over their children. Believe it or not, despite speaking with my children daily, I didn't hover. There were times when Ian and Rhea implored me to step in because they couldn't accomplish what they needed to do. Ian kept losing potential apartment leases when he and his group of three nineteen-year-old college buddies tried to rent an apartment. It became clear that the real estate people were not going to do business with teenage boys. Once I stepped in as a responsible adult, they were able to get a lease. I gave Ian and Rhea latitude and backed them up when they called for it. I viewed myself as a coach at that stage of my children's lives; there to cheer them on.

The truth about how much we missed our children could be heard on our answering machine. It had a message that was taped when Ian and Rhea were ten and eight years old on which each of them took turns saying the message. We didn't have the heart to erase it even if people sometimes told me, "I didn't leave a message because I wasn't sure I had the right number when I heard young children's voices."

Nick embraced the empty nest challenge in his usual methodical way. He edited our household food-shopping list to delete items that we previously bought for the children. Chicken fingers, Gummi Bears, and Jell-O were out and replaced with a thoroughly adult rated shopping list that included humus and brie. Once our refrigerator came of age, I went out on a limb and suggested that we might put on our "To-do List, "Remove the child safety locks from kitchen cabinets."

We think that Ian never totally returned from Mardi Gras that year.

THIRTEEN

The Bungee Umbilical Cord

Ian and Rhea's college years spanned 2000 to 2007 with one over-lapping year. I have referred to this time as an empty nest but that isn't exactly accurate. It was a faux empty nest because they bounced back during summer and mid-year breaks. My cousin says that a couple isn't truly free until the kids move out and the dog dies. By his definition, Nick and I weren't "free" when Ian and Rhea went off to college, by either indicator. Their childhood rooms were kept frozen in time as museums of their youth and our house was still their launching pad. There was also the lingering pet factor. When Rhea was ready to leave for college, she had a fish tank, turtle tank, and birdcage in her room. I became the sole custodian of Rhea's pets while she was away. I was charged with the care of the five family cats, two goldfishes, one rescued turtle, and a parakeet (in a pear tree).

I would like to report that I handled the delegation of pet responsibility well, but that would be less than truthful and I don't want to fall into the false memoir trap. One of the fish was a carnival goldfish that came to us in a plastic zip-lock bag. He started out in a fish bowl that he began to outgrow and, as averse as I was to fish tanks, I gave in to getting a small tank with filter, light, and gravel. Rhea and I maintained the tank together and bought a tank mate for Fishie B. The carnival goldfish was thriving and reached his third year in our care before Rhea left for college. Our hale and hearty Fishie B and his tank mate died within a month of her leaving. I hated to make that call to Rhea. Then came the decision as to burial on land or at sea. I thought the compost bucket offered more dignity than the toilet bowl.

The turtle was a wild turtle brought into our house by the cats when his nest was disturbed by construction next door, near the canal. I was in favor of taking him to the local preserve, but Rhea insisted on getting a turtle bowl. The turtle soon outgrew that environment and we bought a ten-gallon tank with filter and rocks. We purchased turtle pellets and turtle treats. He was the next to take ill. I fought valiantly to keep him alive. The last thing I wanted to do was to give Rhea another condolence call. I bought reptile vitamin spray to spritz on his food and a product called "Dr. Turtle." When that didn't work, Rhea took him to a vet on her winter break and got a shot of Vitamin B and an antibiotic for him. It was not successful and the turtle joined the fish in the outdoor compost bin.

The last of Rhea's pets when she lived at home was a bird. We had no business having a bird in our house with five cats. One of our cats made it his life's mission to have his way with that bird. He sat on the roof outside of Rhea's window and watched him. We had to keep the door to her room tightly shut to keep the cats away from the cage. We name the bird Doot-Doot after the sound he made. He was a delightful little parakeet who chattered intelligibly, saying "Hello, Doot-Doot" and "Doot-Doot's a good boy." Nick taught him to say, "Hello, Nick" in a baritone voice. I find that ironic. I spent all of the time changing the bird's water, feeding him, replacing his bird seed stick, and letting him out of the cage to fly, while Nick just stuck his head in the room once a day and said, "'Hello, Nick.'"

Rhea decided to get a dog to live with her in the house she rented in Miami. We tried to dissuade her, but it was our own fault because she was raised around animals, and she didn't feel like a house was complete without a pet. Her visits home included bringing the dog, a teacup Chihuahua. Monty quickly became our granddog and Nick took him for walks on our block, introducing him proudly to the neighbors while boasting about how smart and well behaved the dog was. Smart and well behaved or not, our little granddog made a mess when he came for a visit. When he was a puppy, we had a wee-wee pad in the family room and it reminded me of the old days when we had the children's potty-chair in the living room.

Nick and I watched the dog when Rhea went away and we were worried that he wasn't eating. A three-pound dog can get sick very quickly from not eating. We found ourselves fork feeding him. We bickered about caring for the dog the way we bickered about caring for our children. One of the most incredible debates we had was over whether it was all right to let him hump his toy bear. I knew my daughter didn't want to encourage the dog to have horny leg humping behavior, but Nick thought it was acceptable for Monty to hump Teddy. I suggested switching to a toy that he didn't love quite as much; Nick thought that would cause him undue frustration. I wouldn't argue if you labeled us crazy. Melanie's husband did, and it sounded so much stronger in Yiddish: "I'm glad to know you two are still 'mashugana.'"

The bungee umbilical cord almost snapped when Rhea decided to discover her Jewish heritage by taking an all-expense-paid trip to

Israel through an organization called BirthRight. I received a call at five a.m. on the day she was due to return.

"Mom, I love it here and I want to stay another few weeks."

"Where would you stay? How would we pay for it?"

"I met this really great guy who was our armed guard, and he said I can stay with his family."

"Rhea, you should come home on the plane as planned. If you want to keep in touch with this young man, you can invite him to the United States," without his Uzi, I thought to myself.

"Mom, don't you remember how you traveled through Europe and Mexico and went to South America having so many adventures?"

"Yes, Rhea, I do remember and that is exactly why I want you to get on the airplane *right now* without any further discussion!" Plane boarded. Crisis averted. Rhea remembers the phone call slightly differently. She recalls that I dangled the offer of buying a car for her so she could get a job and go out with friends when she came home.

Ian and Rhea became more critical of our home after going away to college and spending time with friends at their homes. Ian said he wanted to apply for an internship at one of their houses so he could learn about their well-organized homes.

"It's hard to keep our house orderly with all of the pets and the plants," I answered defensively.

"And don't forget the antiques. I haven't sat down on a chair in anyone else's house and had it fall apart!"

It's true that one of our one hundred-year old dining room chairs fell apart when an out-of-town guest sat on it at my mother-in-law's birthday party. I smiled apologetically and explained, "We're in the process of taking the chairs one by one to the Furniture Doctor for re-gluing and bracing. I guess that's one we haven't gotten to yet."

"The antiques present special challenges," I told Ian, "but it is so worth it when you look at how beautiful and interesting they are."

Ian made the empty threat, "When I have a home it's going to be completely furnished with Formica." It's interesting how the pendulum swings. In the 1950's Formica was the modern look. When I furnished my house, I decided that antiques were timeless and rejected trends that I knew would become outdated.

On one of Rhea's visits home, she informed me that her new boyfriend was meeting us back at our house when we returned from picking her up at the airport. I asked his name and repeated it several times to commit it to memory while I raced around the house with the vacuum to suck up tumbleweed cat fur. Nick's pragmatic approach was, "Tell me when I have to learn his name." He didn't want to waste any precious neurons remembering a name that might be a flash in the pan. My morning radio station was talking about Oblivious Dads. To prove a point, the program intern got his father on the phone and asked his Dad how old he was. The father "guessed" 19 or 20, when the correct age was 21. Men don't waste brain cells on trivia like that.

Within minutes of meeting Rhea's new friend, who was of legal age to drink, Nick suggested they should go out to the garage to choose a cold beer from the refrigerator out there. This male bonding moment didn't seem to require knowing a name. "Oh, no, Nick! Not the garage!" I pleaded through gritted teeth. All of my sprucing up was for naught. The garage is the inner sanctum of our house. There is a mat at the entrance that reads, "Man Cave." Nick has a set-up for planting seeds with potting soil and manure spread out on the table in the center. The kitty litter used by five cats was in the furnace room that is the passageway to the garage. "Not the garage, not the garage!" Rhea's friend chose a beer that Nick served him in an iced mug and he told Rhea that he thought our house was awesome.

There was a debate when the children's love interests visited us as to whether or not they should be allowed to stay in the room with them when we knew that they slept together at school. My parents' generation took the approach that, regardless of what you do when you are away, "When you are under my roof you follow my rules." I tried that. I always made up the foldout couch for guests, but it was never used. I eventually stopped going through the motions. In our prudish culture, children feel as uncomfortable around outward displays of affection by their parents as parents feel towards their children's displays of affection. My friend has three children and, if her husband playfully pats her on the rear end, they hear a chorus of "Get a room!" from the kids.

When Ian and Rhea came home on vacations, the commotion upset the balance that Nick and I had established. Although he would never admit it, Nick was jealous of any time taken away from his reconstituted role as the main object of my attention. I found myself back in the position of family peacemaker. That's when I read one of my other refrigerator magnets, "If we can put one man on the moon, why can't we put them all there?"

One morning, Nick started to cook bacon to make bacon and eggs only to reach for the eggs and find that Ian had used them all and left the empty carton in the refrigerator! All of us were licensed drivers but I was the one who said, "It's not a big deal, I'll hop into the car and drive through Dairy Barn to buy some." Nick could have turned off the burner and gone to get the eggs himself, or we could have awakened Ian to get them. I knew it would be far easier for me to fix the problem.

It is a personality trait of mine, maybe a learned feminine behavior, to want to smooth everything over and be the peacemaker. I remember that as a child, when my mother burned the pancakes, I volunteered to eat them so that no one would make a fuss. My family began to think I liked my pancakes burned and my mother would say, "Here's a burnt one for you, honey." It was a natural progression for me to adopt a "peace at any cost" mediation role between my husband and my children. It's amazing how effortlessly I slipped into that mode when the kids came home to roost.

An amazing development occurred at this time; Ian and Rhea were on their way to becoming their own people and we began to enjoy their company on an adult level. There's a saying that, if you are lucky in life, friends become family and family becomes friends. It was against the odds and without our realizing it, that our family became friends on this journey. The four of us would spontaneously catch a movie or go out for dinner. We had a "docket" for joint outings. As my children pointed out, most people would refer to a "social calendar" and only their lawyer mother would talk about a family docket.

One Broadway show we went to see as a family was Avenue Q. I could not have imagined while watching Oscar the Grouch and Big Bird on TV in 1985, that in 2005, my family would go to see a Broadway show with Muppet-like puppets acting in very adult ways. One curmudgeonly puppet sang the tune "The Internet is for Porn," definitely not Sesame Street material. Our life journey took us down Sesame Street and around the corner to Avenue Q.

The University of Miami had a family weekend that we attended. Rhea was living in Miami with her four housemates and Ian flew in from New Orleans to join us. We strolled through Coconut Grove by day and experienced the glamour of South Beach at night. Rhea brought us to a restaurant in South Beach that was frequented by the "beautiful people" who were dining in the shallow part of the pool with candelabras on their tables. Ian puffed on a twenty-dollar Dominican cigar and sipped fifteen year old Scotch. I had to ask, "Who is this person in my son's tee shirt and what has he done with my son?"

While living away gave Ian and Rhea an opportunity to enrich their experiences, it was not always smooth sailing. There were times when they were each painfully lonesome and I spent many hours consoling them about setbacks, and encouraging them about their great potential. It's easy to gloss over that fact as I look back through the lens of time but it was definitely there.

New Orleans and Miami had a common characteristic of both being rich music scenes. Music, which had been a bond for Nick and me, became an important part of our family's interactions. Rhea chose a school major in music business and entertainment. Ian became an aficionado of music from rap to rock with a special love for New Orleans jazz. We had family playlists which Ian insisted had to be unanimously approved. He was upset when we included a song that he thought was too pop, but when it played on July Fourth and everyone at the house preparing for our big barbecue began singing and dancing to it, it won him over to our side, if only because he liked to see us all having such a good time. Nick and I enjoy being introduced to newer music and Ian and Rhea appreciate music from our era. I was overwhelmed with emotions at a James Taylor concert at Jones Beach that we attended together. As a nineteen-year old lying on the bed in my college dorm, I would not have imagined that someday I would be sharing the same musical experience with my son and daughter.

When Rhea graduated from college, she came back to live on Farmers Avenue for one summer, but her lifestyle and ours were no longer copacetic. She called me from the train station in a panic late one workweek night, when I was already asleep, and informed me that her car had been stolen. I threw on some clothing, grabbed a folder containing her car lease, and drove to the train station . . . where I found her car in the parking lot. I called her on her cell phone and asked her to describe where she was; it turned out she was at the wrong train station. Alcohol was involved. Shortly thereafter, Rhea found an entry level job in Manhattan and I enthusiastically offered to subsidize her rent until she could earn more. She moved into a four story walk-up apartment in the East Village, and Monty, the teacup Chihuahua, remained with us.

Ian stretched his years in his beloved New Orleans to five by staying one year beyond his graduation. He paid a deposit to attend Tulane Law School so he could continue living there but began to have misgivings about his decision. He made a list of Pros and Cons for leaving New Orleans and coming back to New York. His girlfriend at the time, was listed in both Pro and Con columns. He ultimately decided to take a spot at Brooklyn Law. Ian left New Orleans one month before Hurricane Katrina devastated the Big Easy. The apartment where he had lived was inundated by water like most of the city. Ironically, Brooklyn Law took in the Tulane Law students from New York who were displaced from their studies by Katrina. Pros and cons debate aside, Ian apparently was destined to be in Brooklyn. He moved into an apartment style dorm with other students and never came back home to live, but he was a frequent visitor with his friends.

When the kids came bouncing back home, my "To-Do List" included "Eat the burnt pancake, make guest bed that will not be slept in, and manage the family 'docket.'" By 2007, both of our children were settled into their new lives away from Farmers Avenue and Nick and I had to make the adjustment.

Our life journey took us down Sesame Street
and around the corner to Avenue Q.

THE JOHN GOLDEN THEATRE   AGLDAQO81205E
252 WEST 45TH STREET   921192655519
AVENUE Q
$96.25 $96.25 *
TA   8:OO PM FRI   TAAMEX TA
062605   AUG 12, 2005
ORCH   XAWEB1290 0626 C49V   ORCH
*INCLUDES $1.25 FACILITY FEE
P 106   NANOS, LINDA G   P 106

FOURTEEN

The Way We Were

Having the house to ourselves allows a renewed sense of free- dom to sleep-in and walk to the bathroom less than fully clothed. Life plays some cruel tricks on us. One of them is giving us the freedom to have loud, raucous sex anywhere in the house or streak naked when the desire to do so is no longer there. When there were children at home, we had to be discreet. We patiently waited until they were asleep to start romance, not wanting to trauma- tize them.

The morning radio show invited listeners to call in experiences of catching their parents in the act. My favorite was the person who came upon her parents naked and up against the dresser in their room. When she asked in shock what was going on, her father answered that he was helping her mother push the dresser. In their household from that day on, sex became euphemistically known as "pushing the dresser."

Romance is not quite what it was before the children were born. In those days, we couldn't get enough of each other. Gail Sheehy, author of the classic book <u>Passages</u>, published a new book for her generation entitled <u>Sex and the Seasoned Woman,</u> which develops the premise that older women have more fun. I consider myself to be seasoned, though less piquant and more pickled. We had a cat who used to sleep with us, but at the first signs of intimacy on our part, she would jump off the bed and face her head into the corner. I can't say as I blamed her; it's no longer a pretty picture, but that's why God gave humans eyelids and man invented light switches.

Over a course of years, there is always a question in a relationship of how much sex is right for a couple, and it usually isn't the same for both parties. One counselor told us that three times a week for a married couple is "the Major Leagues." Using this analogy, Nick wants to be in the play-offs and I'm content to be on the farm team. After giving birth to Ian and becoming a mother, my changing hormones, as well as the changing of roles, all contributed to the loss of interest in romance. I knew that if I didn't get off the disabled list, I risked being traded. Fortunately, I was relieved to regain my libido and get back on the roster, but never to the extent that Nick would like. I once bought Nick an anniversary card, which explained that the reason men get married is to have someone to blame for not getting enough sex. He sent me a link to a study that men should ejaculate at least 21 times a month to avoid prostate cancer. I questioned with equal gravitas and scientific curiosity whether this could lead to carpal tunnel syndrome.

Most married couples have their established routines. One member of my group says that her husband "makes a reservation" that helps her to get in the mood. He'll ask her if there is room in the inn that evening. Some couples have a regular Saturday night or Sunday morning date. Spontaneity is compromised for the sake of the security of knowing what can be expected from the relationship. Long-term relationships suffer from the lack of excitement of the unknown and imagined potential, but there is a comfort in having a regular squeeze over the long haul. There is one person on this planet who knows the exact spot where my back always itches. While writing this sentence, Nick walked over and spontaneously scratched my back in that spot.

As we age, our bodies are fighting off free radicals (that grab electrons in our bodies, not occupy Wall Street), the ravages of chocolate obsession, and the worst culprit, gravity. I don't understand Nick's continuing fascination with my breasts as a perpetual novelty despite the sagging brought about by all these years of gravity. Breasts have undergone so many trends that I can still hold hope "sagging" is up and coming. In the 1920's women bound their bosom for a washboard effect. Voluptuous made a comeback in the era of the pin-up girls of the forties; pointy high breasts popped up in the fifties, only to be reduced to Twiggy's pre-pubescent look in the sixties. If you follow the evolution of the Mattel Barbie Doll, you can see her body image change. Barbies have gone from lanky, tiny waist, big bosom models to short and curvy regular girls to build confidence and self-esteem in young gals who can never achieve the former Barbie body type. If Mattel would only introduce Saggy Boob Barbie, it might help my generation become more comfortable with our body image.

Exercising could counteract some of the effects of gravity, but I haven't been good about physical exertion. When Nick and I met, I was jogging regularly, playing tennis, and teaching yoga. It seems like a lifetime ago. With Nick's encouragement to get back into yoga, I signed up for a class. I bought a mat and workout outfit, which I was afraid might be too much pressure on myself. I remembered how, when my father took up bowling, we bought him a bowling ball with a monogrammed carrying case for his birthday. Shortly after, he stopped bowling. He walked into the bowling alley with his

167

monogrammed carrying case and everybody would look at him and say, "This guy thinks he's hot stuff. I bet he can't even bowl a spare." Then when he blew a round, people gloated. I overcame the performance pressure and struggled to get back into a more flexible condition, even if not a perfect lotus or headstand. I invited Rhea to the yoga class and she was quick to point out the sign that advertised it as "Yoga Over Fifty."

For those who want to be beautiful but don't have the discipline to exercise, there is always plastic surgery. I was in a doctor's waiting room recently and picked up a copy of "Long Island Beauty Guide" complete with a comprehensive beauty glossary. Since when did we need a glossary to discuss beauty? My curiosity was piqued so I flipped through the pages and learned how I can regain "natural" beauty through facelifts, eyelid rejuvenation, liposuction, Botox, microdermabrasion, and micropigmentation. I can now speak knowledgeably about autologous fat, which is the fat that is transferred from the buttocks to re-contour the face. Though fascinated, I decided to pass.

My weekly appointment at the beauty salon is one effort I make to keep up my physical appearance, albeit not one that challenges my cardio-vascular system. It may be that this salon ritual was firmly ingrained in me from childhood because my mother also had a weekly beauty parlor appointment. In my mother's day, this meant that she came home every Saturday with her hair teased to its fullest extension and sprayed to a crisp.

For several decades, my mother dyed her hair red like all her peers. Women of my grandmother's generation put a blue rinse into their gray hair but red, apparently, is the new blue/gray. The prevalence of red-haired senior ladies always had me doing a double take to see if my mother just walked by. I have thought that my mother was getting short-changed because she was a natural red head and all of these others were imitations. My mom looked very classy when she finally went naturally white. I think back to the time when I started my career and actually wished for gray hair to look more distinguished. I now hate that gray and wash it away, but I haven't yet joined the red hair set. I still go for a chestnut brown and even walk on the wild side of highlighting.

There is a unique relationship established between the beautician and customer. The beautician hears the story of our lives and we of theirs in weekly installments. For well over a decade, I went to Joan who operated a full service salon in her detached garage. It was a place where I would bump into neighbors and exchange gossip with them as well. The beauty salon is like the communal well where news is swapped, and confidences are kept.

My Group surprised me with the fact that all of us had relationships of up to fifteen years with beautician confidantes. We all agreed that our salon visits are better than therapy. The beautician is a great sounding board, having no emotional involvement and no hidden agenda. She possesses a wealth of accumulated information to bounce back at us and sometimes gives us insight through the questions that she innocently asks. Aspiring therapists might save on years of university study, and instead, become licensed cosmetologists. A downside to this relationship is that, if it stops meeting our needs, changing to a new salon or beautician can be like a painful break-up.

When Joan began to set up my next week's appointment, I told her I would not be making it because I was going to get my hair done elsewhere. She said, "I thought we were BFF's." Did I think it would be easy? One time when I had my period and she was waxing my legs, she caught the string of my tampon and, when she pulled back the adhesive strip, my tampon came out with it. That probably qualifies for being BFF's, but best friends or not, I needed a more regular schedule. She was a sole proprietor who changed her schedule every month and had nobody to cover for her when she took vacations or had medical problems. When I wanted to normalize the friendship part of the relationship, I was never fully able to get past that strain.

My roots, regarding hair (and these days, I do mean roots), emanate from a youthful culture in which hair was celebrated as in the musical Hair that encouraged us to let it flow, let it show, as long as it can grow. Now there is a culture of hair loathing. I have used razors, tweezers, depilatories, waxing, and laser removal. There was a time while living in Mexico in the 1970's when I stopped shaving all together. It was very freeing for me, but when I returned to the United States, my resolve was broken by the penetrating stares I received causing me to break out in a sweat. Once my beautician was waxing my leg and went for my big toe. When I reacted in shock, she explained that it had hair on it. "Well," I told her, "that's because I'm a mammal. It happens." The hair was removed under protest.

There is one hair growth that has never been in style for women, and that is the chin whisker. When the sun is especially bright and I put my car visor down, in the mirror I may spot a chin whisker that escaped my tweezers in the house. My morning radio station invited listeners to call in particularly disturbing activities they saw taking place in other vehicles on the road. I need to police myself and confess to my own offense. I carried tweezers in my car and I have pulled out these randomly occurring chin hairs, at a stoplight. Laser hair removal has eliminated this disturbing behavior.

Women are not alone in these hair wars. It is some consolation that Nick also battles unwanted hair growth. When Nick goes for a haircut, it now includes his ears and nose. Nick is also gray these days, which for a man includes gray facial stubble. Here's a Zen Koan: "What do you call a five o'clock shadow when it is white?"

My salon routine includes manicures. It surprised me that I, Ms. Earth, Wind, and Unshaved Legs, became Ms. Hair and Nails. For a good part of my life, I bit my nails and cuticles. I finally broke the nasty habit when I saw Rhea following my example. I couldn't scold her about biting her hands without being a hypocrite. It reminded me of a Gandhi story. A woman brought her child on a long day's journey to see Mahatma. The child was obese. She asked Gandhi to tell her son to stop eating sweets. Gandhi instructed her to come back the next week. At a great hardship and inconvenience, she repeated the long journey to see Gandhi the following week and asked again for his assistance in dealing with her child's obsession. Gandhi replied simply, "Young man, don't eat sweets."

The mother dismissed her son and then asked, "Mahatma, please forgive me for questioning because I know you are all wise, but I must ask why you did not tell my son this last week and save me the repeated journey?"

"Because," he replied, "last week *I* was eating sweets."

I began to set an example for Rhea. I can proudly report that Rhea and I both now have lovely manicured nails! For a time, I was having my nails done by a Chinese manicurist who didn't speak much English. I felt uncomfortable not interacting with her so I asked her to teach me a phrase in Mandarin each week. I learned how to say "Nails look beautiful" in Mandarin, which could come in very handy if I ever travel to China.

While I got my hair and nails under control, my weight has been my nemesis since my first pregnancy. After Ian was born, I joined a weight control program and achieved lifetime membership status.

This requires me to weigh in monthly at within two pounds of my goal weight. Mercifully, my goal weight has been adjusted each decade to be more realistic. Even so, I go through ridiculous measures to weigh in under my goal weight, like wearing linen drawstring pants when there is snow on the ground. Despite the games I play with myself, it keeps me somewhat on track but not ready to wear a two piece bathing suit.

I have a paperweight that says, "It could be worse. We could be trying on bathing suits." My fashion style could be described as "Smoke and Mirrors." Scarves around the neck and Spandex blend pants with tummy control. When it comes to bathing suits, all of the cover-up is stripped away. My make-up includes under eye concealer, which I also put on the deep creases of my wrinkles in other areas of my face to soften their appearance. When you put it all together: hair, nails, make-up, weight program, mature wardrobe, it amounts to a high maintenance miracle of illusion.

I honor my body as the temple of my soul and accept that my temple requires this upkeep. I can't say the same for Nick. The Dalai Lama teaches to be kind, whenever possible, and follows with the observation that it is always possible. I would be kinder to Nick if he were more realistic but, in his mind, he is still the college wrestling champ weighing in at 115 pounds. He started our relationship as a buff, tanned beach boy and now, with white hair, sun-weathered face, and ample gut, resembles Ole Saint Nick. Fortunately, Ole Saint Nick is a huggable guy.

When Nick was scheduled for a medical exam that was required to purchase more life insurance, the agent asked over the telephone how he would rate his physical condition. Without hesitation, he answered, "Prime." I'm sure Nick wasn't taking into consideration the fact that he needed a hip replacement, a full set of dental implants, a label on the shampoo bottle with marker so that he can find it without his glasses in the shower, and an amplifier for the doorbell. Other than that, he was in tip-top physical condition. When we were rearranging our bedroom and had to move a heavy full-length mirror, Nick pulled out a tool from his carrier that locates beams in the wall so that we could hang the mirror securely. As he moved the stud finder along the wall, he muttered in frustration, "I can't find a single stud in this room." I was about to say, "Ditto" when I remembered: be kind whenever possible; and it is always possible.

One morning, I remarked on how long Nick was gargling with Listerine. I thought it was quite impressive since I can't hold the stuff in my mouth for more than ten seconds. He said it is because he is so "macho." That's my husband; leaps over buildings in a single bound and gargles with Listerine for twenty seconds! He has also started to turn off the hot water at the end of his shower to get a blast of cold water to stimulate his thyroid. I hear him braying in the bathroom, which is quite sexy in a primal kind of way.

One of our friends invited us to a "The Way We Were" party. She asked us all to dress as we did in the seventies and to provide a picture from that decade in advance of the party. When we walked into her house, she had a bulletin board displaying all of our pictures. She devised a game in which we were asked to guess the identity of each person and then vote on the most and least changed. Nobody could identify Nick and me; the years had really taken their toll. We had each gained thirty pounds of flesh and lost a few pounds of hair. I only prayed to not be voted "most changed." We each received one vote in the category of most changed. Nick was certain that I had cast that dreaded vote. I swear I didn't (that's my story and I'm sticking to it).

The mind is also in on the conspiracy of degenerating faculties and functions, with my brain on a thirty-minute delay. Ask me any trivia question and it will be on the tip of my tongue, but not on my lips, for at least a half hour. Suddenly, I will blurt out a name, five conversations later. The polite smile I get doesn't nearly acknowledge the feat that I have just accomplished of dredging up a long forgotten bit of information. I actually do exercise my brain, more so than I do my body, by working on crossword puzzles, but with smart phones, it is even easier to skip the memory exercise. Nick and I were trying to remember the name of a country singer. We knew one of us would come up with the name eventually, but then I reached for my phone and asked it for the answer. I worry what will become of our minds now that we don't have to recall any facts.

We took a meditation and mind control program called Silva Mind Control back in the late seventies. One of the sayings that has stuck with us for all of these years is a mantra about becoming "better, better, and better" every day. If someone asks us how we are doing, they are likely to get the shortened reply, "better and better." Since our physical attributes and memory are not improving, you may wonder what is. I can say that we are wiser and kinder, and that counts. We appreciate the gift of our lives and are grateful that our physical bodies are healthy. Despite the self-deprecating humor, which is all in fun like the Way We Were party, we love each other and ourselves. If you spend time with us, you may also hear Nick's signature "Love you live" when he says good-bye. It is a more positive spin on the expression, "Love you to death!"

My personal grooming "To-do List" today is preoccupied with controlling natural mammalian hair growth: "Dye, cut, pluck, shave, wax, zap." I vote we should bring back the sixties to revel in hair growth, wear billowing Dashikis that cover all evils, and conveniently blame our lack of memory on being stoned.

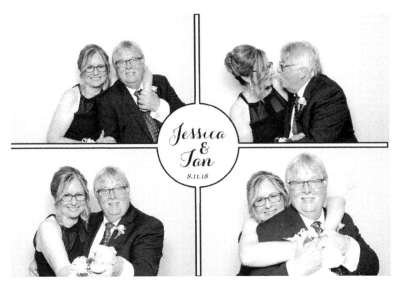

We appreciate the gift of our lives and are grateful for our physical bodies.

FIFTEEN

"Lock the Doors"

One skill honed with age is the art of coping. The year 2018 got off to a terrible start, so much so that a friend hugged me and said, "You have a right to be depressed." After all, we had two family funerals within 3 weeks of each other, my office was flooded, my two staff attorneys were on maternity leave at the same time, and my daughter broke up the band by moving 1700 miles away. Nevertheless, I had to question the concept of a right to be depressed. I have heard of the inalienable right to a Pursuit of Happiness immortalized in the Declaration of Independence, but a right to depression isn't protected and probably shouldn't be. There is nothing to gain from the immobilization caused by depression. I cry when I am sad and shout when I am angry, but then I get on with the business of my life.

Life is a series of challenges and we are defined by how we deal with them. I have experienced this in my personal life, as a lawyer listening to the struggles that my clients face, and as an employer who is told the reason why an employee needs time off to handle an individual or family problem. We can careen through life like a ball in a pinball machine hitting the tilt button or take charge of how we maneuver through these obstacles, but one thing is certain, there will be obstacles and sometimes, very serious ones.

I want to take a moment to distinguish between tragedy that is network evening news worthy and setbacks we all encounter. They are not in the same category, however, my observation of people who have channeled their energies into constructive movements and foundations in the aftermath of tragedy leads me to believe that, even in those circumstances, taking action has a healing effect. I have lived through national tragedies and a natural disaster. People of my parents' generation remember when the Japanese attacked Pearl Harbor. My generation remembers where they were when President Kennedy was shot and can recount in detail the events of September 11, 2001. For me, 9/11 had a particular impact.

In 2001, Nick and I were both gainfully employed in our own businesses. I moved my office to a bigger, more professional location with a comfortable size staff of ten. Any time I felt stressed, Ian would try to comfort me by saying, "Mom, you're a small business owner, not the President of the United States." The move to my new office was in July 2001. We had just finished a huge immigration program and there were many others on the horizon. As they say, the future was so bright, I had to wear shades.

Two months after I moved my office to the new location, the terrorist attacks of September 11, 2001 devastated the whole nation and changed our world. There is a spoken word song based entitled, "Everybody's Free (to Wear Sunscreen)" in which Baz Luhrmann, in 1999, spoke about the futility of worrying. He explained that the real troubles in life are not likely the ones you worry about but things that blindside you on a Tuesday. I was driving to work that Tuesday morning, preoccupied with thoughts about the cases I had to deal with, when the radio began to report what was happening in

Manhattan. Who could ever have imagined the insanity of someone flying a plane into a building? Then another! We watched the buildings implode from the roof of my office in Hempstead. All of our worlds imploded that day.

I was fortunate not to lose anyone whom I knew personally, although we had a few close calls. I had an attorney from the office who was in downtown Manhattan at the immigration district office that morning. We always used the World Trade Center subway stop to get there. The government building was evacuated and my employee trekked by foot uptown to try to get a train out of Manhattan. By late in the day, he made it to his apartment on Long Island and collapsed from emotional and physical exhaustion. He later learned that a dear friend of his perished in the towers.

I had another employee whose husband was a fire marshal in Manhattan. As my staff watched the drama unfold from the rooftop of my office building, she was distraught. Finally, someone called to say her husband had been seen on television running away from the building as it was collapsing. In the months that followed, he had the task of identifying his comrades by means of personal articles retrieved from the site. His work at ground zero resulted in his needing an organ transplant years later.

I loved the World Trade Center. When I attended a conference there, I was so in awe of the building that I called Nick from the lobby and described everything around me. I remember saying, "This is how the other half lives!" The final scene of the novel I wrote about the Salvadoran man uniting his family took place in view of the World Trade Center as a symbol of optimism. That symbol of optimism became a symbol for one of the most heinous occurrences in human history. I was heartbroken and couldn't walk past a picture of the Twin Towers without crying.

Tears are important for the healing process, but there is an Italian proverb that says, "Never a wedding without tears or a funeral without laughter." For a time after 9/11, New York's "Saturday Night Live" suspended its broadcasts to be sensitive to the overwhelming grief. When the show was ready to go back on the air, they invited New York's Mayor to the show. The Producer asked the Mayor in the opening act for permission to be funny. The Mayor quipped, "Why start now?" What a relief it was to have my first heartfelt laugh! Up to that point, my only moment of comic relief was when my associate called her mother upon hearing about the attack and said, "Lock the doors!" If only it were that easy to keep evil at bay.

In the Billy Crystal memoir, 700 Sundays, he reminisces about the Cold War days when the Communists were our archenemies. We had "duck and cover" drills in which we curled up into balls with our heads against the wall in school to practice bracing ourselves for an attack. Did some official actually think this was going to prevent us from disintegration in the event of an atom bomb exploding on New York City? I can remember trying to pull my skirt down over my thighs so that my underwear wouldn't stick out as I huddled on the floor. My teacher admonished me that I would not be worrying about my underwear if the Russians attacked us. She had bought into the Cold War hysteria wholesale.

If the business of government is to protect its citizenry, then enemies are good for business. For my parents, the Japanese and Germans were our enemies, only to become our allies post WWII. In my lifetime, we have feared the Russians, Cubans, North Koreans, North Vietnamese, Iranians, and Iraqis. We invaded the tiny island republic of Grenada in 1983, although I never figured out who or what we were supposed to be afraid of there. After the 9/11 attack, the government developed a very useful Color Coded Alert system to let us know if we should be severely panicked or just mildly worried. I don't know about the rest of America, but when we hit Code Red, I'm going to "lock the doors" *and* "duck and cover."

The wave of xenophobia following 9/11 had serious implication for my immigration practice. All of those wonderful programs that were cooking in the oven during a time of peace and prosperity were placed on the back burner. The government and INS turned to an anti-terrorist campaign. It was not a good time to be an immigration lawyer helping foreign-born to make their status in the U.S. legal.

My personal and business finances were characterized by yo-yo prosperity. Nick urged me to find a new way to make a living, the way he himself had done years before, but it was unfathomable to me to leave the law. Nick's next suggestion was that I should at least change my area of practice. It was not that easy for me because I had developed a clientele and an expertise over a long period of time. I didn't want to begin again as a novice, and most importantly, I loved immigration law. I have a sign over my desk at home that says, "Show me your faith apart from your works, and I, by my works will show you my faith." If immigration law was my calling, it would not do to leave my calling to be answered by voice mail.

The type of immigration law I practice is known as humanitarian. I handle defense against deportation, applications for asylum, relief for victims of violent crimes, and waivers based on extreme hardship to citizen and legal resident relatives. In hardship cases, I do an analysis of all of the factors that will impact on the U.S. citizen or legal resident family member: medical, financial, psychological, family ties, education. One couple was consulting with me and I asked whether their baby, asleep in her carrier seat, had any special needs. They answered, "Yes, she was born without eyes." I felt as if the wind had been knocked out of me and took a minute to regain my professional composure.

I have represented deaf clients with a sign language interpreter and blind clients. One of my clients was a severely handicapped man. While guiding him down the stairs to leave the building, a security guard said to me, "You're doing good work, Counselor." Mother Teresa said, "We can do no great things, only small things with great love." I don't provide solace to the untouchables or live my life with a vow of poverty, but I do my best to earn a living assisting people who really need help. I tell my staff that we are changing people's lives one case at a time.

You don't need to be in a helping profession to have a profound impact on others. You can do random acts of kindness in any walk of life. I read a biography of a woman, Jane Welsh Carlyle, who was a literary socialite living in England in the 1800's when women weren't permitted to work or own property. She socialized with the likes of Charles Dickens and Ralph Waldo Emerson but, more than being a highly respected socialite, she wanted her life to matter. She made it her mission to help displaced women find placements in homes as nannies or tutors. She saved many women from being destitute without ever being gainfully employed.

In the aftermath of 9/11, my office was teetering on the brink of collapse, but that was a deep, dark, debilitating secret. I was recruited to serve on the Board of Directors the Nassau County Bar Association, one of the largest suburban associations in the country. The glaring-eyed Dean of St. Johns Law who used to frighten the briefs out of me also sat on the Board; one of those ironic twists and turns of life. I was invited to be an advisor to the local Congresswoman, an honorary member of the Central American Refugee Center, and a Trustee of my religious congregation. I created a program for the local Bar Association to increase the diversity in both our membership and the community served, and I accepted an award on behalf of our association from the State Bar for that program.

From outward appearances, anyone would have thought my career was running on all cylinders when the truth was that it had blown a gasket. The recognition didn't translate into income for my office when there were no programs that benefited my clients. The word bankruptcy floated through my head and I found myself sinking into a depression that made it difficult for me to go to work some mornings. It is socially taboo to discuss personal finances so we don't know how many others are struggling with financial problems and often they will only speak of it, as I admittedly am doing, after the crisis has passed. I overheard a neighbor telling Nick how he had to withdraw most of his life's savings to keep his business running the prior year. In a memoir by my former partner, Ed, he wrote that his assets and income plummeted in the aftermath of the financial crash in 2008. I never heard about it at the time and only knew he had decided to down-size to a smaller home.

It is a little known fact but lawyers top the list for incidence of depression among 105 professions. I might have guessed that. Nobody ever says, "Happiness is a law degree." Two out of three Americans who suffer from serious depression are women. As a female and a lawyer, the statistics were stacked against me. I have known both loneliness and depression, and if sometimes I speak lightly about difficult topics, it is only to make them more palatable to ingest and easier to discuss. Women exhibit anxiety, physical symptoms, and internalized emotions when faced with depression. Following the suicide of fashion designer, Kate Spade, the New York Times cited the frightening CDC statistic that, since 1999, the rate of suicide among women has increased 80 percent.

The advice for coping that one most often hears is to take one day at a time. I took one moment at a time. A seeker once traveled the world over looking for the meaning of life, "Was it a matter of making ends meet until we meet the end, or was there more to it?" Someone directed him to a guru in the Himalayas. He entered the cave and found the guru sipping a cup of tea. The seeker asked the guru his burning question. The guru answered, "This cup of tea is the meaning of life. A moment ago is gone; the next moment is not here yet. All anyone has is the moment at hand." I comforted myself by thinking, "Nothing bad is going on right now. I'm in my car listening to music and the sun is out. This moment is just fine, and this moment is all there is."

When I encountered a new snag at work, I reminded myself that there is stress in any job. In the 1950's, we used to have vendors selling door-to-door. Most women in those days didn't go to work and the typical household had only one car, which the commuting husband took to his job. We had milkmen, Fuller Brush cleaning products, Avon cosmetics, and one of my family's favorites, the Dugan cake vendor. All brought their products to the housebound homemakers. The Dugan man once told my mother he was having a stressful day because he brought our neighbor her usual coffee ring only to have her capriciously decide, that day, she wanted a crumb cake. When he brought her the crumb cake, she didn't like the way it looked and asked for Danish. It was a regular caketastrophe.

I never did declare bankruptcy, but the light of hope at the end of my tunnel turned out to be a flashing Strobe light. While my law practice was floundering and Nick had become a steady financial contributor to the family, it became necessary for him to schedule a hip replacement. Nick came through the hip surgery full of optimism for his recuperation. He ordered a walker with a tray on which he could place his acupuncture needles, so that he wouldn't have to be out of work for a prolonged time. He knew his contribution was needed.

During Nick's stay in the hospital and rehabilitation, I visited daily, bringing newspapers, bottled waters, get-well cards received at the house, extra-wide sneakers with Velcro fasteners, sweat pants, and anything else that he required or desired. What really frightened me was the prospect of having to provide care for him at home, by myself. Never in my childhood aspirations did I hope to be like Florence Nightingale. I respect the nursing profession; my mother being a nurse, but it wasn't one of my goals.

We fixed the bathroom with the special equipment needed, including a bench in the tub with handles to grasp and I set about the task of giving Nick a bath. It was a luxury to him, especially after the long stay in the hospital, to be lovingly bathed. He made a special request for me to wash his feet, reasonable given that he had been wearing high-pressure support socks every day. After bathing, drying, and dressing him, he sat down at the kitchen table where I served him lunch and brought him his paper, water bottle, and the telephone. I was thinking that he must feel very embarrassed about his care needs, but instead, he leaned back and said, "I feel like a King." That made me not the loving wife but the chambermaid.

These were times when I felt that "for better or worse" was truly put to the test. Every day before I left for work, I had to dress Nick in his underwear, pants, and shoes. Some days, I left early and Nick didn't have to be up until 10:00 so, on those days, he had to sleep for a few hours with his shoes on. One morning he called me at work when he got up to say that I had put his pants on backwards. I apologized but told him it would be impossible for me to get away from the office to come help him. He had to wear his pants backwards all day and was feeling less like a King and more like a Court Jester.

After Nick's hip surgery, we visited Melanie's mom, Shirley, who had also undergone a hip replacement. Nick and Shirley began to exchange joint replacement stories. Before I knew what was happening, Nick dropped his pants to show my eighty-something family friend his scar. Her health aide fled from the room. I screamed for him to stop mooning my poor Aunt Shirley, but she told me not to worry about it. She said she wasn't shocked by anything Nick did and it was the most entertainment she had all week.

If you are keeping track of hardship, there is one we haven't touched on yet, so let's add the natural disaster to the mix. Super Storm Sandy slammed the Atlantic Coast in October 2012 and we had a storm surge of three feet in our house. The entire first floor was destroyed. The house smelled like a clam bed at low tide. I used a crow bar to pry open the china cabinet that held gold trimmed Lenox bowls and platters, and crystal glasses we received as wedding gifts. I poured the canal water into a bucket, vessel by vessel.

We heaped furniture and belongings in a mound at the curb, same as every other neighbor for as far as you could see. I watched through our window as the woman who had cleaned our house for many years stopped by the pile of destroyed belongings that she had painstakingly dusted, polished, and scrubbed. She covered her face in her hands and her shoulders shook as she sobbed. She collected herself and came inside not knowing I had seen her grief. I salvaged my antiques and sent them to be refurbished. We lived at the house of our guardian angel friend, Martha, while our downstairs was gutted.

These are the times when you can appreciate the support of people around you who face adversity with you. More often than not, we need to get by with a little help from our friends. Once we had heat, hot water, electricity, and no more sparks shooting out of outlets, Nick and I moved back to our house in a makeshift apartment upstairs. While I was coordinating contractors and completing paperwork for the insurance company and FEMA for our home, I was doing the same for my aunt.

I evacuated my Auntie Annie from her house in Long Beach the day before the storm and brought her to a hotel. Her house, also located next to a canal, was devastated. She had been a meticulous housekeeper and bookkeeper. I found a ledger from the 1950's of every household expense and bill paid. The ledger was spared on a high shelf. It was best that she never re-visited her house. I reached into a pile of belongings to get a vase and I had ringworm on my arm the next day. Working with FEMA, I was able to find and fund a temporary residence for Auntie Annie in an extended stay hotel until my cousins and I could get her into a nursing home.

My Auntie Annie's mentality was forged by living through the Great Depression, World War II, and discrimination against Jews and career women. She achieved a stable and secure life for herself but was always waiting for the other shoe to drop. When her best friend hemmed her pants and asked her how she liked them, she replied, "So far, so good." The friend asked, "Anne, what are you expecting to happen?" The storm was the other shoe dropping. Losing her home and lifestyle at age 95, she only survived six more months. She was collateral damage of Super Storm Sandy.

Years later, water proved to be my nemesis at my office as well as at home, leading me to consider the law of attraction as explained in The Secret. The book states that your thoughts manifest themselves in your life. I have thought verbalized the idea of being "swamped" at work so often that it should have been no surprise when I arrived at my office to find water cascading from the ceiling with my desk in the middle of a lake that spilled into the hallway. Files were literally floating around in it, "swamped," so to speak. A toilet had broken on a floor above us. My staff and I got to work rescuing soggy files from the deluge and spreading them out to dry. The landlord called in a restoration crew. Only six months prior, I had closed my office for floor to ceiling refurbishing and here we were rolling up our sleeves again.

Wayne Dyer said that we are spiritual beings having a human experience. We are on this planet to feel joys and sorrows, highs and lows. I have faced crises in my marriage, finances, career, ailing elders, and a natural disaster. It was all manageable adversity. When I feel blue, I try to do something thoughtful for someone else. I stay in the moment; I don't disasterize the problem with words like "never" and "always," and I narrow the focus to the problem at hand. Every challenge along the way has expanded and shaped who I am. Joni Mitchell wrote in the lyrics of "Woodstock," that she didn't know who she was but life was for learning. Sometimes, I hope that I have learned my life lessons and that I have had my quota of hardship (if such a thing exists). Perhaps I am due for some coasting. My "To do List?" Put up my feet and relax.

We heaped furniture and belongings in a mound at the curb,
same as every other neighbor for as far as you could see.

SIXTEEN
"Smile, Bob"

Let me set the stage for a memorable moment that demonstrates how I can, unintentionally, aggravate my husband. We host a sit-down dinner for over twenty guests every Thanksgiving. One year, I scraped all of the turkey and meat table scraps from our guests' plates into a container to feed to the cats. I failed to label said container. When I looked for it the next night to supplement the cat kibble, I learned that Nick had eaten it for lunch and fed it to the kids as well. In another Thanksgiving cat-related incident, my sister-in-law, Tricia, was helping with the holiday cooking and asked the simple question as to whether or not we feed raw meat to our cats. Simultaneously, in stereo and without missing a beat, Nick answered, "Yes" and I answered, "No." I told Tricia she could take her pick, whichever answer she liked better. It is truly amazing how Nick and I can be out of sync so often.

During our relationship, our work schedules have greatly reduced the tension between us. I have worked days, Nick has worked nights and we both work Saturdays. Maybe couples who can peacefully spend every minute together are soul mates. I marvel when I see husbands and wives out shopping together. Nick and I wouldn't agree on where to shop much less what to buy. Does that mean we are not soul mates? Not only do we not finish each other's sentences, but half of the time, we cut each other off and contradict one another. Maybe the true definition of soul mate is the person who most knows how to push all of your buttons.

In a class I took on Improvisation, I learned to pick up on the last thing said with the phrase, "Yes, and..." to keep the scene rolling in a positive direction. Another course in Compassionate Communications taught us to reflect what the other speaker was feeling to show we understood what they were expressing. Once I was washing dishes and Nick needed something from under the sink. He bumped me aside. I said, "Use your words." He replied, "Get out of the way." I said, "I was looking for something more like 'excuse me.'" We laughed until we cried. No number of communication courses can prepare you to react to that. Someone once referred to Nick as a diamond in the rough. I think his carbon molecules need another million years of heat and pressure.

We have a friend who was convinced that her recently deceased husband was sending her signs. I gave her the book to read in which two life partners suffering from AIDS agree that whoever dies first would send the other a sign. Nick asked me if I wanted to make the same agreement. We made a pact that whoever passes first will annoy the other from the grave, and in this way, we will be certain it is a signal from the other side.

Some people say, "Never go to bed angry." I will admit to going to bed angry on many occasions, but we try to wipe the slate clean each day and begin fresh. We have coffee together and read the newspapers in the morning. We talk about our plans for the day. When we are grooming and dressing is when I like to share the book

I am currently reading with my Book Club. Nick gets to hear about it chapter by chapter.

Sometimes, when I am telling someone about the book, Nick corrects a fact.

"Didn't that book take place in New Zealand, not Australia?"

"Oh yes, you're right," I answer.

The person we are talking to will ask, "You read the book also?"

"No," Nick replies. "I heard it on Books by Linda."

We have dinner with each other most evenings. I try to get home in time for the evening news. While listening to the news, we get teary-eyed at the same stories. During baseball season, we root for our favorite team and have a drink. In the summer, we spend beautiful evenings at concerts in Jones Beach Theater. I feel contentment in these shared experiences.

Our bonding comes, in part, from the fact that we haven't forsaken those original hippie sentiments that were an attraction for us in the beginning. We surround ourselves with plants and animals, keeping close to nature. Our love of music keeps us dancing in our seats at concerts. One of Ian's friends observed that we belong to that "love everyone" church, which features a stained glass display with symbols of all of the world's major religions. Nick and I are both involved in careers that help to better other people's lives, sometimes to the exclusion of our own material gain. Yes, admittedly, we are aging hippies-guilty as charged.

Back when I was starting both my law practice and my family, a young CPA approached me about giving my office account to him to manage.

"What type of car do you drive?"

Caught off-guard, I answered his intrusive question. "A Toyota Corolla."

"And what type of house do you live in?"

"I don't think I like where you are going with this."

"Humor me."

"Okay, a Cape Cod."

"If you hire me as your accountant, I can almost guarantee that you will be able to move out of that Cape Cod and trade up from your Toyota."

I hadn't considered the fact that my life's circumstances were so deplorable. I was outraged to the point that I suggested to the CPA's boss that he might want to give a second thought to this new associate he had hired. Since Nick never planned to move from our little Cape Cod, we had to re-invent it numerous times to suit our needs. It came to be like a Lego house where we slapped on additions: a new living room, a larger family room, a master bedroom, a greenhouse, a front porch. Remodeling, renovating, and repairing required first mortgages, second mortgages, and refinancing, giving personal meaning to the concept of "the money pit."

The Town of Hempstead provided me with five feet of front lawn when it raised our sidewalk and put sod on the yard it had disturbed. Nick wanted to dig it up, but I guarded my five feet of sod with a lethal grass clipper. I eventually got a porch with bric-a-brac and two Victorian wicker rockers on it. I had managed, through great effort and at times literally against the tide, to make the house, which Nick had bought with his ex-wife, my own. With our last building permit, the Town of Hempstead advised us that we had reached our yard usage limit. Unless we were going to put on a third floor, I believed our renovations had ended. I was mistaken when we had the unscheduled and unanticipated renovations arranged by Mother Nature. I added up all of the money borrowed for our many renovations and paid out by our flood insurance and arrived at the conclusion that we lived in the one million-dollar Cape Cod on a dead end street which I now, out of respect, refer to as the "cul-de-sac."

The influence of the Loom of Life is strong. Like my mother and father before me, I find myself feeding wild birds these days. I have five outdoor feeders that I fill with seed every morning by 6:30 a.m. and I sprinkle cracked corn on the ground around the bird bath fountain. We are visited at our waterfront by up to fifteen bird species. My mother used to complain about her bird feeding that, "All I get are brown birds." We have cardinals, blue jays, green Monk Parakeets, and, most wonderfully, red-winged black birds. I have attracted to my own yard that beautiful sight that thrilled me as a child riding on horseback. It is another reminder of the law of attraction. What you visualize will be. Ironically, Nick asked me who was going to feed the birds when we were going away overnight. My parents would be proud!

I found Nick's original posters from Woodstock rolled up in the back of his closet and framed them as a Christmas present. One poster hangs in our kitchen, next to our picture on the WNEW listener calendar, and the other in our den as daily reminders that we are card-carrying members of the hippie generation, a dwindling breed. Soon they will have to gather us up and put us onto preserves for endangered species. There we can continue undisturbed and regardless of the trends in the larger society, to compost our organic waste, listen to classic rock, and sing along to "Alice's Restaurant" on Thanksgiving and "All Things Must Pass" on New Year's Day.

Hippies like to name themselves after celestial objects like Starshine and Moonbeam. We would have to choose new names that reflect our true nature. Most heavenly bodies are made up of dust and gas, both very familiar to me. I would pick a name that I think has a nice ring: Swan Nebula. Maybe Nick might grow his ponytail back and I could revert to wearing herbal deodorant because my life will be so stress free that I won't need twenty-four hour antiperspirant protection. It's a harmless fantasy.

Nick and I have fallen into a routine of taking off from work on Wednesdays since we both work on Saturdays. He refers to them as "Naked Wednesdays" but that is not true (well maybe they were once or twice). Our neighbor calls it "Bathrobe Day" because he sees us picking up the newspaper in our bathrobes instead of seeing Nick and our Chihuahua, Monty, kissing me good-bye when they walk me to my car. We begin Wednesdays with a yoga class in Nick's office in view of lush, pink bougainvillea flourishing on the highest shelf in the greenhouse. It wasn't lost on me that one of the peak times of my life was practicing yoga in Cuernavaca next to the pink bougainvillea. To have recreated this in my home on Farmers Avenue is meaningful. Nick and I have begun to say, "These are the good ole days."

Wednesdays are also my day for appointments, errands, and a weekly dinner date (all done fully clothed). I was standing in the bank one Wednesday when I stopped what I was doing and told the teller, "That's my wedding song playing on the radio." It isn't one that is played very often, so I listened to it all before going back to making my deposit. It's a song by the group Genesis, "Follow you. Follow me." The sentiment is to follow each other and stay with each other for all the days to come though we can expect one tear in every year.

I have to say there was more than a single tear in each year, but there was far more laughter. Call us sentimental old fools, but Nick and I cry at weddings. At one friend's wedding, we were surprised to find that their minister was the one who married us! Nick took my hand and we walked over to him.

"Jim, we're Linda and Nick. You married us back in 1979."

"Well, how about that! I guess I can count you among my successes," he said shaking our hands. "Do you have any advice I can share with my newlyweds?" he asked.

Nick's advice was, "Learn these two words and say them often: 'Yes, Dear.'"

Mine was, "Lower your expectations."

We seek a mate with certain preconceptions. A woman needs a man who is kind and understanding. A woman needs a man who is a good provider. A woman needs a man who is funny yet romantic. A woman needs a man who is intelligent and an engaging conversationalist. Ideally, *these men should not know each other*! All kidding aside, it is unrealistic to think that your mate can be all things to you all of the time. If he manages to be some of them some of the time, then I would consider that you are ahead of the game.

In a quirky book by Wayne Dyer, <u>Gifts From Eykis</u>, which he said in his 1984 letter to me was "his life's mission," he writes these beautiful words on relationships:

> There is really only one sure way to make your relationships work, and that is to recognize each other's right to be separate, unique human beings without any "ownership" expectations from each other.

Reading that made me even more embarrassed about telling Wayne he was "not attainable," as if one can "attain" another.

In the book <u>Notorious RBG</u> about the life and times of Supreme Court Justice Ruth Bader Ginsburg, the justice recounts the advice her new mother-in-law gave her for a successful marriage, "It helps sometimes to be a little deaf." I have found that to be true in marriage as well as motherhood. There are times that it is better to act as if we did not hear something because the ones we love sometimes say hurtful things in a thoughtless moment. In another part of <u>Notorious RBG</u>, the Justice's husband states that the most important role he had was to let his wife do what she has done. I always felt the freedom in my relationship to do what I wanted with my life. We each have been able to pursue our interests and support one another in reaching our goals, despite our spats along the way.

On my parents' fiftieth anniversary, Ian said, "I don't think you and Dad will ever get divorced because both of your parents made it to their fiftieth wedding anniversaries."

Indeed, our heritage gave us good prospects. At their fiftieth anniversary party, my parents renewed their vows at a ceremony officiated by my brother's wife. When my sister-in-law initially told them she was studying to be a minister, they were embarrassed to share this news with their Jewish friends. To their credit, they stood before all of their friends and relatives renewing their vows with a Christian minister. My parents celebrated their sixtieth wedding anniversary at the senior community. Only five per cent of all married people make it through the obstacle course of life and marriage to reach their fiftieth wedding anniversaries, and I imagine that the percentage drops dramatically in regards to the sixtieth.

My father succumbed to Alzheimer's and eventually had to move into the dementia unit in their retirement community. My mother visited him every day, but as she began to leave, he would get his electric razor and begin to go with her. It was sad to leave him behind but she couldn't manage his needs. He asked the doctor the rhetorical question, "Shouldn't a husband sleep with his wife?" That was a tough one with no acceptable answer. I was thankful that my Dad seemed to still remember who I was when I visited. It's true I never tested him and always announced who I was, but his face lit up when I entered the room. My father passed while living in the dementia unit. My mother survived him by nine years, but had a life-ending cerebral hemorrhage on what would have been their seventy-fourth wedding anniversary. Theirs was truly a love story for the ages.

Having buried three elders over the past decade, I have a deeper appreciation for the importance of human touch because, once that vehicle of the soul is gone, that is what you can never have again. The spiritual being lives on in memory but the physical is no longer there. Robinson Jeffers, in his "Inscription for a Gravestone" wrote, that upon leaving his body, he wandered in the air, leaving only a precipitate of ashes to earth as a love-token. I make sure that I touch Nick every morning before I get up by holding his hand or placing my hand on his chest to feel his heart beat because one day we will be a precipitate of ashes.

Nick's parents separated not long after their fiftieth and their relationship can stand for the idea that it is never too late to change the course. I remind Nick of that when he annoys me too much! His father never understood why his wife left him; as he put it, he "let her go to Bingo." I guess that over-indulgence was his big mistake. How 'ya gonna keep 'em down on the farm, after they've played Bingo?

It was more than a little awkward to have his mother and father at holiday gatherings together, not knowing how to act towards each other. At first, his mother made up a plate of food for her estranged husband as she had done for fifty years. After several years of separation, they eventually just greeted each other and shared news about a friend or relative. When he died, she sat with her children in the first row at the wake.

I was reminded of a Bob Dylan concert at Jones Beach Theater that we went to years ago, when he projected his trademark carrying-the-world-on-his-shoulders demeanor. I thought, "Smile, Bob. We made it through so many tribulations and we're here by the water on a beautiful summer night listening to music." With Mom and Dad gone and the children on their own, life is a little less hectic. I have more time for myself. I go out to dinner with my life-long friends, Melanie and Janet, at least once a month and get away with them for a weekend every year. My house is more orderly and the underwear is once again folded in the drawers. My marriage has been challenged at times, but I am glad we are still together.

For anyone considering divorce, freedom from challenges of a relationship may seem appealing at first, but seventy-five percent of divorcees re-marry. That tells me that marriage is still the preferred lifestyle. The appeal of marriage is across the board of social class, including among the rich and famous. The NY Times wrote an article about "serial grooms" who marry repeatedly, because either they like the institution or they want the trophy brides. Either way, these perennial husbands are willing to shell out millions in prenuptial payments to set themselves free, only to marry again. The article explains that marriage provides respectability, status, and comfort, and maybe even love, for awhile.

There are many people who do not choose divorce but it is forced upon them. We cannot change how others feel or act, we can only control how we respond. Janet was thrust into a separation that was not of her choosing but she responded with strength. She had a career and bought a home where she raised her daughters, and eventually, shared her life with a new partner. She maintained a friendship with her former spouse and promoted good relations between him and their daughters. This is the best that anyone can do under those circumstances.

For a time, I didn't think either of my children would marry, but Rhea found a wonderful guy, Kris, who loves not only her, but also our unconventional family. He is smart and funny. He wants to be counted in on the family docket. We found a new activity, archery, where we can be aggressive and competitive, and have fun doing it!

When Rhea began to plan a wedding, I made one small request: please don't have an outdoor ceremony. The guests nearly always end up being uncomfortable because it is too hot, too cold, too windy, or rainy. Bless my independent-minded daughter. She decided to have a farm wedding that included a ceremony under a noble, old tree and a reception under a tent. The farm was a gorgeous, pastoral setting with fields, woods, and a backdrop of mountains. It was also fairly rustic. A bit of inherited hippie-ness was coming out in her.

We spent the day leading up to the wedding stringing lights. One of my projects was to make paper bag lanterns by filling white lunch size bags with stones to weigh them down and placing battery operated tea lights on top of the stones. I positioned *seventy five* of them lining the driveway down to the ceremony area. I rolled up eighty shawls and placed them in a basket in case the temperatures dropped down as predicted in one report ten days prior to the event. I ordered an extra tent for the ceremony so that we could take shelter if it rained. We had air-conditioned rest rooms brought onto the farm. I tried to think of my guests' comfort in every possible scenario.

The meet and greet Friday night alongside a pool was terrific, especially when Rhea was singing along with her husband's band

and they were joined by a full New Orleans brass band, a surprise arranged by her new brother-in-law. In the early morning hours of Saturday before the wedding was to take place, it rained. All of my paper bag lanterns collapsed into wet garbage that had to be gathered and trashed by the wedding planner later that morning. The ceremony was sweet and personal, officiated by a friend who had become ordained for the occasion. We escaped further rain, but the heat was oppressive. My Honest Abe friend, Melanie, told me she spent a part of the reception cooling off in the air conditioned portable bathrooms. During the party, I borrowed the microphone to encourage guests to take home a shawl to wear *on some other occasion* when they might actually need it.

Rhea was a beautiful bride and danced the night away. She later told me that we had given her and her husband the wedding of their dreams. It was an exercise in stepping aside and allowing my daughter to be her authentic self. She sent me a picture taken on her honeymoon wearing a wrap-around Hawaiian print skirt and turquoise stone necklace that I had given her, and as she put it, channeling me. There turns out to be a great deal of me in her authentic self. She has become a Social Media maven with impressive credentials. She may have inherited my career ambitions, but not my ineptitude with media. Her quote is, "Ugh, parents on Facebook."

Ian was slow on the social maturity track, but he has moved towards full adulting. He is an in-house employment lawyer in the financial services industry with an apartment overlooking a tree lined street in the East Village of New York City. His fiancée, Jessie, redecorated the apartment and rid it of the oil painting of monkeys playing cards. They have a car, a dog, and an upcoming wedding. Jessie is a sweet and beautiful addition to our family who has joined the family text chain and the family docket.

Everyone becomes an adult at his or her own pace. I know that I didn't wake up one day as an adult; it was a long process. When I turned fifty and my mother turned eighty, I realized it was high time for me to stop sharing my problems with her. From that moment on, our roles reversed and I became her caregiver. In her nineties, I picked her up every Sunday to take her shopping or on any errands that she needed to do. My mantra was "No regrets." Although she was 96 years old when she passed, her death was unexpected with no time for good-byes, so I was thankful that I had no regrets.

After my mother was gone, the last of her generation in our family, I realized that I am now the older generation. Neither of my children shows any interest in having babies, so I will stop the book short of the grandmother experience. The cycle of this book is complete with my daughter marrying. Her generation can now experience the childbearing years, or not. Women have fought hard to have lifestyle choices and that is one of them.

At their fiftieth anniversary party, my parents renewed their vows at a ceremony officiated by my brother's wife. Theirs was truly a love story for the ages.

SEVENTEEN
"Scoot Down"

Hormonal overtones have affected my career in tandem with my personal life. My first law office, Yang and Nanos, produced four babies in five years and spawned a tradition that spilled over into my subsequent law practices. An associate who started working with me as a paralegal when she was 21 years old became a lawyer, but before she passed the Bar exam, she had her first baby. She went on to have three more while working for me. I took on young female interns from a paralegal program and offered jobs to them after their internships. Many of them worked with me through marriage and children.

I might have related to them a bit too much. I dreamed about the pregnancy of a paralegal who had been working for me for nine years. In my dream, she was sitting next to a pool watching her young children play in the water. There was such a strong maternal vibe in the dream that I came in the next day and asked if she was expecting. She wasn't aware of being pregnant until about a week later when she was late for her period and her pregnancy test came back positive.

My office was abuzz with hormones of as many as ten female employees. Each was afraid that I would have an emotional meltdown when told of a new pregnancy, knowing the coverage headaches it invariably presented. I always remembered to congratulate them on the good news before going into my office to scream. My office saw my employees have ten babies over a ten-year period. The culmination of this trend came when I had two thirty-something female attorneys become pregnant at the same time! I have heard of women who live together menstruating at the same time, but getting pregnant at the same time? I found that the employees bonded over the baby showers and sending each other pictures of their new babies.

When one of the attorneys returned to work after ninety days and had a need to breast pump, we were faced with the challenge of how she could make court appearances. On her first day back in the federal building, she visited the General Service Administration office and found a civil service employee minding the shop. She asked him for a private space to pump her breasts. By the amount of stammering that ensued, it was safe to assume he had not previously faced this request. Now when she appears at his door, he nonchalantly escorts her to a private conference room.

It is not all progress in the world of working women. It was disappointing to read in a New York Times article in 2018 that many of the country's most prestigious companies still systematically sideline pregnant women, passing over them for promotions and raises. Only thirty-six per cent of practicing attorneys are women, according to the American Bar Association and their salaries are less than that of men. We've come a long way, Baby, but still have far to go.

One trend I am pleased about is flaunting the Baby Bump! The young women in my office wear form-fitting tops through their ninth month of pregnancy with pride. I would like to see Mattel come out with a Baby Bump Barbie. The only problem is that Mattel announced, in 2004, that Ken and Barbie grew apart and separated so we would have to find her a new significant other. I would help design Baby Bump Barbie's wardrobe to be as different as possible from the maternity clothes of my generation.

Maternity blouses and dresses of my day were huge tents with polka dots and bows at the neck. I never understood the style, but I think it was supposed to be demure. In 2018, my attention was riveted to a car spokesperson in a television advertisement who was obviously pregnant. I realized that I had never seen a pregnant spokesperson on TV. What should be startling is not that this was on TV, but that it had never been before. The most natural human phenomenon, at the root of all of our very existence, has somehow been hidden off screen. I was a little disappointed that the spokesperson did wear a polka dot maternity top.

I have watched the employees in my office become beautiful mothers. I am flexible about their need to take off for a school conference or doctor's appointment. None of them abuses the accommodation. They are in communication with the caregivers who are watching their children and the children's schools during the day. I honor their juggling of work and parenting as someone who has been there and done that.

It was not easy for the one male paralegal I had on staff for a year. Whenever another male came into the office, whether it was the mail carrier or the copy repairman, I observed that this paralegal established a sports conversation within minutes. "Did you see the game last night?" I would hear from the file room. It was a relief for him from talk of children and husbands. I would have happily discussed baseball with my male employee, but I don't have the right jargon.

Nick often asks me what happened in the baseball game if he didn't get to see it. I say things like, "They won in overtime." He sighs and shakes his head back and forth slowly. "How many years have we been watching baseball together?" he asks. "You mean they won in 'extra innings.' There's no overtime in baseball!" I understand why my paralegal waited for the testosterone to arrive.

While all of my young employees were taking turns giving birth, I began to have hot flashes. You cannot be inconspicuous when you are hit with a hot flash; it feels like a train coming through. It wells up from the solar plexus, past your short-of-breath lungs and into your burning ear lobes. I continually shed my suit jacket, hanging it on the back of my chair, until the damp perspiration caused me to feel a chill, and then put the jacket back on. The clients must have thought I was very strange. My doctor told me I could be in that declining hormone condition for several years before the final onset of menopause.

At one point, I stopped having periods for at least six months and I was sure that I had moved on to the new phase of life. Nick wanted to help ease the transition so he prescribed an herbal regimen three times daily. The hot flashes stopped, but I began to have regular periods again! I really felt as if I was too old to be menstruating; it almost felt a bit ridiculous. If I continued with the herbal regimen, I would have had to rename this book "Fifty Years of PMS." Unbeknownst to Nick, I reduced the dosage to once a day. It managed the hot flashes, and I did reach the destination of menopause on schedule.

Like my mother before me who kept a baby stroller in the garage to keep from getting pregnant, I may never throw away the boxes of tampons in our bathrooms for fear I will menstruate again. Besides, you always have to be prepared for a guest who may need one. Amy Schumer did a routine on Saturday Night Live about being out to lunch with a group of women and mouthing the word "tampon" whereupon every gal at the table reached into her bag, and suddenly, she had a choice of size, brand, and degree of absorbency. It's part of the sisterhood "The Sisterhood of the Tampon."

Although I no longer had to mouth the word "tampon" in desperation, I was still on a quarterly check-up basis. Even when the routine is familiar and you have been through it countless times, there is an "ab initio" sense of humiliation. When you put your feet in the stirrups, invariably the GYN follows the words "scoot down" with "relax." It is not easy to relax when a cold metal speculum is inserted between your legs.

In this discussion of female medical care, we can't forget the need for us maturing women to have mammograms on a regular basis. I am good about my annual mammograms, mostly because my mother and grandmother had breast cancer. Every time I endure one of these exams, I think the same thing: a man had to have developed the mammography procedure because no woman would ever come up with a plan that involves squishing breasts between cold plates.

At my most recent mammogram appointment, I found a totally new approach at the radiologist's office designed to make the experience more pleasant. Mammography patients were directed to a newly decorated salon with piped-in music, couches, and a table with a plate of cookies on it. Once the procedure was underway, I told the technician that it would take more than cookies to make me think I was having a good time. I suggested dinner and wine might do it for me and I would help to promote it with the slogan: "Enjoy a dish as we squish; drink some Merlot at your next Mammo."

The topic of mammograms was raised at my Group and we all shared our harrowing experiences. The prize went to one of the women who is less than five feet tall. She said that she has to stand on her toes to place her breasts on the plates and, once they compress, she literally hangs from the mammography machine by her bosom. We decided she should bring her own step stool with her the next time.

In addition to mammography, I also needed regular pelvic sonograms. I was on a first name basis with the nurses at the radiology group. When my appointment was on St Patrick's Day, I promised to come wearing green underwear. A pelvic sonogram is another extremely unpleasant procedure that requires drinking a quart of water and holding it in while pressure is applied to the pelvic area to view the uterus from all angles.

My doctor thought I was taking a risk with my life by not having a hysterectomy. I told him he was the best doctor I didn't ever listen to. We reached some mutual understanding and I feel I struck a reasonable balance. I wasn't being irresponsible. I had blood tests, biopsies, and pap smears. There was an article in Newsday reporting that 600,000 hysterectomies are performed in the U.S. each year. With those numbers, there should be a new line of get well cards in the store racks for "Wishing you a speedy recovery from your hysterectomy".

Fewer than ten per cent of hysterectomies are for cancerous conditions. Most are for benign conditions such as fibroids or endometriosis. The hormone devastation that follows ovary removal leads to increased heart disease, a great danger to women. Heart disease kills more women over sixty-five than all cancers combined. The Newsday article also mentions, almost in passing, that women report a loss of sexual pleasure after having a hysterectomy. This point is rarely spoken about to women and was verified by a friend of mine who confided to me that she did find sex to be less enjoyable after her hysterectomy. I am not a medical doctor, and I am not telling women to ignore their doctors, only to discuss their options and make an informed decision.

There is a common female experience that has been treated as a socially taboo topic, miscarriage. My niece, Janelle, is a journalist for The Boston Globe and wrote an article in 2015 entitled, "Why We Need to Talk about Miscarriage." She shared her own painful experience and the fact that it is such a hush-hush subject, that when a woman endures a miscarriage, she is usually unaware of just how common an occurrence it is. I am not advocating the overshare equivalent of streaking emotionally naked down Main Street but I think honesty is the better route than making a cover-up story for the miscarriage.

Women need to bond over hormone issues. What a wide range of experiences: menstruating, PMS, ovulating, birth control, pregnancy, post-partum, lactating, miscarriage, hysterectomy, perimenopause, menopause, and coming back full circle with hormone replacement! We have pap smears, pregnancy tests, mammos, and sonos. It would be so boring to have nothing more to talk about than the last sports game we watched. We should be eternally grateful for the variety of hormonal experiences we are treated to over the course of a lifetime; men miss out on this spice of life!

The male of the species is less challenged by his anatomy. There's the obvious physiology "toilet-seat-up/toilet-seat-down" dissimilarity. Women are taught about putting toilet paper down on the seat in a public bathroom from the time they are old enough to urinate on their own. No man has experienced the humiliation that one of the women in my Group experienced when she returned to her classroom to teach with her makeshift toilet paper seat liner hanging from the back of her pants. Men are equipped to take care of their business quickly and easily; my mother used to say that men have a "picnic gadget." If there is any truth to penis envy, it occurs when a woman at a concert compares the length of the line to the women's room with no line to the men's room.

The differences between the sexes don't stop with outward anatomy. Nerve circuitry for person perception is more developed in the female. One study found that testosterone reduces men's ability to make eye contact, one of the most basic elements of personal interaction. For men, the dynamics are far simpler than for women. When men reach puberty and their hormones kick in, they become horny. During their lives, they exhibit extreme horniness, moderate horniness, and slight horniness. I have asked myself the question on many occasions, what is it about men that allows them to be ready for sex in just about any circumstance?

On Nick's first morning home from ten days in the hospital following his hip surgery, I offered to make bacon and eggs for breakfast. He replied, "I've been away for a while and I'd much rather have sex than breakfast." I gave him a little quiz:

"Nick, answer 'True' or 'False.' You haven't had anything but a sponge bath in ten days."

"True."

"You have an incision clear across your buttocks held together with staples."

"True."

"Your foot and leg are swollen to about twice their normal size."

"True."

"Sorry, Dear, I'm only offering breakfast!"

Many tests have been conducted to try to determine just how often men think about sex. Another study, reported in <u>Psychology</u>

Today, found that the majority of teenage boys had a sexual thought every five minutes. Once they reach their twenties, according to a study reported at a psychology convention, they think about sex around thirty-seven times per week, more than four times as often as women. It is fortunate for survival of the species that there is some overlap with the men during the nine times weekly when women are thinking about sex.

The importance of these hormones cannot be underestimated. They are the driving force behind dating, mating, and procreating. Once those passions subside, another important hormone comes to the rescue, oxytocin. According to National Geographic's article entitled "Love, The Chemical Reaction," oxytocin is a hormone that promotes bonding. It is released when we hug our spouse or children. Our species needs human touch. In marital counseling, some therapists suggest ballroom dancing in order to re-introduce a couple to touching each other. From there, they can advance to healthy marital relations.

Sex plays a vital role in keeping marital partners connected emotionally over the long term of marriage. It's one of the factors that sets this union apart from other relationships. What I haven't figured out is the role that sex plays in our golden years. There is a joke about a man who calls his friend to report with great concern that he thinks his wife is dead. His friend asks, "What makes you think that?" He replies, "The sex is the same, but the dishes are piling up." Geriatric sex doesn't fit into the evolutionary scheme. It seems to serve no legitimate scientific end other than to keep us from killing our mates. Then again, that may be its legitimate purpose. Would any of us put up with all of the flotsam and jetsam of our mates if we didn't need the goodies?

Sixty million baby boomers have passed the half-century mark. Fifty-somethings are more active and vital than ever. It is said that fifty is today's thirty, and that includes sexuality, necessitating a shift in how people view mature intimacy. We are flooded with commercials on television, like ads for Viagra and products to relieve feminine dryness, designed to reassure us that you are never too old for intimacy, but mature intimacy has its own challenges.

Nick's hip replacement was the harbinger of a new phase of our relationship. Our bodies are like our house that was built the same year I was born. The house requires a new roof and window replacement; I anticipate repairs to both house and body are in store for me.

I have a long range "To-do List:" "Write survival guide for the next stage of life." Be prepared with your hearing aids and bifocals because <u>Forty Years of Prosthetics</u> will be available on audible books and in large print for my contemporaries to enjoy.

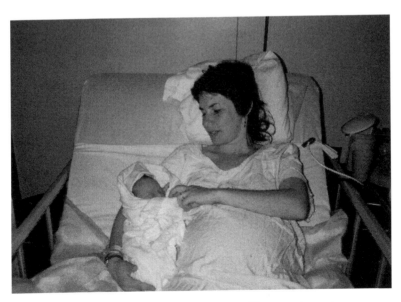

We should be eternally grateful for the variety of hormonal experiences we are treated to over the course of a lifetime; men miss out on this spice of life!

EIGHTEEN

Diary of a Freezer

I began writing this book in 2005 and attempted marketing it for a year or two before abandoning the project. My manuscript was left suspended for more than thirteen years until an unexpected event occurred. Melanie, Janet, and I usually go out for our monthly dinner on a Friday night. Because of an impending trip, Janet asked to get together on a Tuesday night and suggested a restaurant locale closer to Melanie and me. We found ourselves having dinner outside of our normal routine. It turned out it was Ladies Night at the restaurant with half price wine and Tarot readings. The host came to our table and asked if any of us would want to have a reading; I signed up for the entertainment value with absolutely no agenda.

Apparently, I am an open book to any psychic. The reader asked whether I had a question for her. I told her that I did not because I didn't know I was going to have a reading. "That means you were guided to me," she said. She began displaying cards and making very meaningful and pointed comments. Then, she looked puzzled and told me she was receiving a message from a deceased person who was one of her favorite authors and spiritual guides, Wayne Dyer. She told me that she regretted never having met Wayne before he passed but she reads from his book, <u>There's a Spiritual Solution to Every Problem</u>, every night before she goes to bed. She said that Wayne had a message for me: there is a book you need to write. At that point, I revealed to her that I had known Wayne fairly well. I showed her a letter from Wayne that I posted on Facebook when he died in 2015. She and I were both a bit startled. Before she ended the reading, she told me Wayne was again stressing to her that I should write the book before I die.

I know that psychic phenomena is not for everyone. My own son-in-law is a non-believer and I love him dearly, so if you consider this my personal delusion, I won't hold it against you. I didn't want to become dependent on psychic guidance, but I felt compelled to go back one more time. I had two unpublished manuscripts: the novel about the Russian mail-order bride based upon my client's true story and this book. With intention, I made an appointment for a reading and told the psychic that I had a follow-up question to the previous session. All she remembered was that I was the one who knew Wayne Dyer. I asked which book Wayne was urging me to write. She answered, "The one about women overcoming obstacles."

I explained that I had abandoned my manuscript, then entitled "Forty Years of *Menstruation*," many years ago. One agent had been horrified by the title: "Ministration? How could a book about 'ministration' be funny?" The agent not only couldn't pronounce the word, but she couldn't look me in the eye. Her eyes darted about the room as if she were searching for the nearest exit. The psychic replied, "I don't know if this is coming from me or Wayne, but the title should be 'Forty Years of *PMS*.' People will be more comfortable with that." And here we are at the end of my story.

<u>Forty Years of PMS</u> began with an invitation to the reader to a slumber party. You came with the snacks and I brought you into the

kitchen to sit down and have a drink. You probably noticed the display on the refrigerator door. The invention of refrigerator magnets was a break-through innovation that has allowed our refrigerators to be a reflection of our lives, from macaroni mosaic art to college graduation pictures. The door of our refrigerator has displayed report cards and awards, our holiday photo greeting cards, and poignant political cartoons. We had a snapshot of the World Trade Center taken from a friend's boat there for many years after 9/11. We currently have two Save the Date Magnets for two children's weddings.

If the kitchen is the center of family life, the refrigerator is at the epicenter. Family members come through foraging for food on a regular basis and sometimes open the door just to stare in and to see if anything new has appeared since the last time they looked, but a polite guest doesn't go into the refrigerator without being told to do so. More so, a guest rarely opens the freezer because its contents are in deep storage. This book has defrosted many memories from the deep freeze.

I have seen my freezer go through several incarnations, being a storage place for vastly different commodities. In the lost years of the seventies, there was LSD. It was a time for experimentation and exploration that led to finding a mate and preparing a home for our offspring. The eighties found the icebox stocked with more responsible items such as breast milk, fish sticks, and first aid ice packs. Parenting has been on-the-job training from the day I left the hospital with my first swaddled infant and has not stopped to date.

The nineties sprouted homegrown herbs for consumption as well as medicinal purposes as the family adapted to living with Martial and Healing Arts. We managed to keep the family afloat through financial and health crises. The new millennium found Jell-O shots placed inconspicuously in the back of the freezer by experimenting young adults who tested our patience and creative parenting. Today the icebox is the vessel that holds chilled Captain Morgan's rum and flavored vodka for imbibing when Nick and I come together at the end of the day.

My life's partner and I sit across from each other at dinner, having a drink and trying to fathom that we have lived through four decades together. It is hard to believe that I-the mother, the wife, the lawyer, the employer-am the same person as that free spirited twenty-something who sunbathed nude on the roof of a house and *was with friends* who were tripping on LSD in Madrid. Like Dr. Who, I feel as if I have regenerated multiple times, each time emerging as a new individual possessing a database in common with my predecessors. In my lifetime to date, I have purchased Pampers for my children, adult diapers for aging loved ones, and perhaps one day may have to buy them for myself.

I received a Mother's Day card from Ian that listed all of the roles a mother plays for a son. It said that a boy needs a Mom who will be real keen on making sure his underwear is clean; making him eat foods that are right; stopping him from dressing like a fright; sending him to school to learn to be smart; and helping him appreciate theater and art. I felt a sense of relief as I went down the list, reading each one and mentally check marking to myself "Did that, did that!"

When I reached the end of the list, I was equally relieved by what was not on the card. There was nothing about being a perfect homemaker. The son of one of the women in my group remarked when he visited her native Philippines, "My cousins are happy even though they live in dusty homes." My kids could say the same and they weren't living in a foreign country. Maybe the author of the greeting card poem realized that being less than perfect in a traditional role was not as important as being a nurturing mother. I certainly hope that what my family remembers is the love and reliability over the years, through the good times, bad times, and through the many personal changes I have undergone.

Women are strengthened by the need to persevere with the demands of our daily lives, despite the inconveniences of bleeding like a stuck pig during menstruation or sweating like a roasting one through menopause. We may struggle with depression but we don't have the luxury of sitting back and pampering ourselves when our children, our husband, or our parents need us. Alexa, the voice acti-vated virtual assistant, was once directed by Nick to "Forget that. Ignore that command." Alexa relied, "I am not programmed to ignore." Maybe that is why Alexa has a female persona. Whether it was crying babies, meowing cats, or my elderly mother needing to go to Walmart, I was not wired to ignore the needs of my family.

There is a sense of solidarity among women because we share the hormonal phases of life that mark each new stage and challenge us so much more than they do our male counterparts. Erratic hormones are the hand we have been dealt. Having given birth, I can say that it is an incomparable experience. I will never forget the bonding of breastfeeding my babies. There is so much to share and support to be offered. This became abundantly clear as I met with my group. There were pains that I had held for many years that were lifted when I shared and laughed about my life.

Throughout this story, I have reflected on how we weave a cloth from a Loom of Life. While we each have a different fabric, the threads hold our fabric together. Sometimes, the threads were pulled thin and sometimes tied in knots. During my forty or so years of menstruating, I forged an identity for myself that didn't fit into any neat boxes. I was an independent career woman while still being a vital part of my family. I have held a marriage together through some trying times. I can't claim to have lived up to all the feminist ideals of the sixties and seventies. I've admitted to packing my husband's suitcase for him, but I never fully crossed over to the other side of traditional homes and gardens womanhood either. In fact, I have fallen far short of those ideals as well with incorrigible housekeeping and a questionable approach to childcare.

Despite missing the mark as a traditionalist and women's libber, I have taken on the role that women have always had in our society; to function as the glue that holds a family and a marriage together. In the early years of my career, I felt I was venturing into new territory as I found a way to balance family and professional calling. I patented my own brand of adhesive glue for that phase. When all was well and I only needed to orchestrate our busy lives, it was white and flowing like Elmer's. Then I was called upon to be the sole support of my family and my glue became a no-nonsense Epoxy. That glue was less pleasant than the one of my trouble-free childhood memories, the thick, white paste from the kindergarten classroom that smelled so good you can hear the teacher saying, "No, no, Johnny, don't eat that!" More often than I care to disclose, I was making up my craft as I went and it was just plain Krazy Glue. There may come a time when I am old and perhaps senile. I may forget what glue is used for but I hope that others will say I was the bond that held my marriage and family together.

Now it is your turn. What is your glue? What is your fabric?

We weave a cloth from a Loom of Life.

40YRSPMS TALKING POINTS
(AN OPEN ENDED LIST)

ONE: WARNING: ADULT CONTENT

- Your first kiss
- How you lost your virginity
- Ways in which you drove your parents to distraction

TWO: DISCO DROPOUT

- First heartbreak
- A blind date disaster
- How you met your mate; what initially attracted you

THREE: PEPTO BISMOL IN THE WEDDING PHOTO

- How your mate proposed to you (or vice versa)
- A wedding snafu
- Your honeymoon's worst moment

FOUR: THE COMPOST BIN ON FARMERS AVENUE

- One of your mate's possessions that you would like to mis-place, permanently
- Are you and your mate on par for neatness/organization?
- A memorable "getting-to-know-you" fight

FIVE: BREAST PUMPS AND BRIEF CASE

- Bottle or breast
- Child care choices
- Employment during child rearing years

SIX: FROM THE BACK SEAT OF THE GLADIATOR

- What your child might talk about on a shrink's couch
- Characterize your parenting style
- Gender stereotyping your children

SEVEN: TO HUG OR NOT TO HUG: THAT IS THE QUESTION

- Your answer to the question "To hug or not to hug"
- Why you love/hate extended family
- What fabric would your life would be?

EIGHT: DESPERATELY SEEKING DISNEY

- A family outing gone bad
- Cultural experiences you gave your children
- Your strength/weakness in teaching your child

NINE: AT THE BOTTOM OF GOD'S PURSE ...IS CHANGE

- The division of labor in your home
- Maternal sacrifice (yours, your mother's, or your grandmother's)
- A grandma story

TEN: NEEDLES OR NOTHING

- A time when your family's security was threatened

- A time when you stepped up to the plate for your family
- "Relationships Suck"- agree or disagree?

ELEVEN: THE BARF CLAUSE IN THE LIMO CONTRACT

- Fibs you told your children
- Some of the hats you have worn in your household/one that didn't fit
- When did you get "the talk"/give "the talk"?

TWELVE: ADULT RATED SHOPPING LIST

- Life after kids move out, better or worse?
- Cutting umbilical cord, cold turkey or gradual?
- An unpleasant call from your child

THIRTEEN: THE BUNGEE UMBILICAL CORD

- If your children bounce back home, what is that like?
- Do you take the burnt pancake?
- Your child's pet that you took care of

FOURTEEN: THE WAY WE WERE

- The way you were/are
- Ever caught your parents in the act/get caught in the act?
- Live to 120 or death wish at eighty?

FIFTEEN: "LOCK THE DOORS"

- Setbacks you had to cope with
- What coping tools do you use?
- A time when you had to nurse or take care of a loved one

SIXTEEN: "SMILE, BOB"

- What makes someone a soul mate?
- Are you friends with your kids/your mate?
- Is "yes, dear" the answer? Lowering expectations? Ear plugs?

SEVENTEEN: "SCOOT DOWN"

- Your most embarrassing or uncomfortable GYN experience
- Which is worse, menopause or menstruation?
- Silly Wabbit, Sex is for kids

EIGHTEEN: DIARY OF A FREEZER

- What do you want your legacy to be?

ACKNOWLEDGEMENT

I acknowledge Wayne W. Dyer whose influence, during his lifetime and beyond, was empowering to me.